RECENTLY DISCOVERED TALES
OF LIFE AMONG THE INDIANS

Recently Discovered Tales of Life Among the Indians

James Willard Schultz

Compiled and Edited by Warren L. Hanna

Preface by John R. Mauff

MOUNTAIN PRESS PUBLISHING COMPANY
MISSOULA, 1988

Thanks to Hartley Pond and Mike Warren
for editorial help in publishing this book.

Cover painting by Lone Wolf (Hart Merriam Schultz)
Courtesy of Harrison Eiteljorg

Library of Congress Cataloging-in-Publication Data

Schultz, James Willard, 1859-1947.
    Recently discovered tales of life among the Indians /
James Willard Schultz ; edited by Warren L. Hanna.

      p.   cm.
   ISBN 0-87842-221-8 (pbk.)
   ISBN 0-87842-230-7 (cloth)
   1. Siksika Indians—Folklore. 2. Indians of North America—
Montana—Folklore.   I. Hanna, Warren Leonard, 1898-1987.
II. Title.
Egg.S54S318 1988   88-92241
398.2'08997—dc19   CIP

Mountain Press Publishing Company
2016 Strand Avenue
Missoula, MT 59801

Preface

"Recently discovered . . . Literary Find of the 1980s . . . *Tales of Life Among the Indians!*" If Warren L. Hanna so captioned this unique anthology of the early writings of James Willard Schultz of which we are now the beneficiaries, it was no immodest claim on his part. Here is a legacy both of Schultz and of Hanna, who was himself a man of remarkable literary gifts, in many ways a man of personal characteristics that could equally be applied to Schultz: "an insatiable curiosity," "a lifelong interest in things," and having had "a love affair with Glacier National Park."[1]

True, Schultz, a century ago, *lived* these pages that we now relive, and Hanna, his biographer and friend across the years, enables us to do so, to appreciate the similarity in the two men in those traits described above as belonging to Warren. For Schultz too was a man possessed of a great curiosity, of an interest in things, and with a profound love for that part of the magnificent northern Montana Rockies we now call Glacier National Park.

With justifiable pride Warren taps a "treasure trove" for the many to whom James Willard Schultz has come to mean one of the truly great men of the Old West, who indeed proved to be, in Hanna's term, "a Renaissance man." It was not only in the explorations and hunting trips and identification with the Blackfeet tribe within less than ten years after coming to Montana in 1877 that make him what he was and is, but that he became a chronicler of that time and place.

Along with becoming established as a professional writer Schultz entered the arena of advocacy for the native Americans of that part of the country. And like his friend George Bird Grinnell, Schultz through his writings and actions was influential in leading to the establishment of Glacier Park in 1911.

Warren spoke to me more than once of how his path crossed with that of Schultz during the two summers (1918 and 1920) that both were there at the same time, Warren as an employee, Schultz as guest of the Railway. Coincidence, a casual contact, still it developed into a strong admiration by Warren for what Schultz represented and led to the definitive biography of *Apikuni*[2] , a major piece of research in itself and which led to further research the results of which are here for the first time reproduced and made available.

Our friend Warren liked a good story, being himself a lively raconteur. Whether he was a detective story buff I cannot say, but it is clear from his various writings[3] that he had the instincts of a first-rate private investigator. Clues and their pursuit to a final successful resolution form the basis for this collection. During the writing of the biography there were abundant references to certain of Schultz's early writings that were published by the magazine *Forest and Stream* between 1880 and 1894. Schultz was in his early 20s then.

This took some doing, but recognizing the clues, Warren was if anything even more intrigued when he found that accessibility to those issues was far from simple. A good detective likes a good challenge, and in his Foreword to this collection one can follow his quest and sense his growing enthusiasm after he had located where the microfilms could be reviewed, a process that if he were with us would lead him to say: "That was only the beginning!" Somehow finding the time and energy along with his career in the legal field (itself prolific with books and articles on insurance and worker's compensation), he kept on the trail and followed where it led. The end product is an important supplement to his earlier biography, illuminating and documenting a short but significant period in the life of James Willard Schultz as he moved into manhood.

The reader will see it in this light, but also as the splendid homage of a contemporary historian, Warren L. Hanna, whose insights and persistence were and are wholly admirable, to *Apikuni*, James Willard Schultz, 1859-1947, pioneer, explorer, hunter, and author, a figure unique as a paradigm of the exciting era that these Tales so faithfully picture and preserve. Warren referred to Schultz as "a rare and very unique individual." He should have known, for he was one himself.

John R. Mauff
February, 1988

---

[1]*Warren L. Hanna. 1898-1987, A Celebration of His Life* (Program for Memorial Service, October 4, 1987)

[2]*"The Life and Times of James Willard Schultz (Apikuni)* University of Oklahoma Press, 1986

[3]further prime example of his "keen judicial analysis and mastery of historical narrative:" *Lost Harbor, The Controversy Over Drake's California Anchorage*, University of California Press, 1979.

Chronological Table of Contents

From *Forest and Stream* — 1880-1894

Categorical Table of Contents

* From *Great Falls Tribune*; inserted at this point for chronological continuity

James Willard Schultz about 1920.

—Courtesy of Archives, Montana State University Libraries

Foreword

Among writers of Indian adventure stories during the twentieth century, James Willard Schultz has undoubtedly been the best-known. His books were published in this country by Houghton Mifflin, and in a number of countries abroad, including Russia and Israel. His praises were sung by his contemporaries, one of whom called him "an artist of narrative and a master of suspense." Although most of his work was fiction, it was largely based upon the unique experience gained during his years of living with the Blackfeet. Since he died in 1947, it may be too early to assign him a permanent rank among writers in his particular field.

When I was a youngster, the name of James Willard Schultz was well known to countless teenagers, including nearly all of those whose parents subscribed to such magazines as the *Youth's Companion* or the *American Boy*. I happened also to be the recipient of a copy of Schultz's first book, *My Life as an Indian*, published in 1907. The perennial popularity of this fascinating book was such that it went through many editions and sold half a million copies. I still treasure my own, now in my possession for more than seventy years.

My experience as a North Dakota school boy was typical of an ever-widening youthful audience throughout the country — an audience of boys that could hardly wait for the next issue of the magazine in which a Schultz serial was appearing. The arrival of a new Schultz book in a school or public library was eagerly awaited and its appearance quickly known to his young aficionados. Such books were read and re-read until they fell apart, which may help explain why so few copies of his books can be found today, even in catalogues of rare book dealers, and then only at prohibitive prices.

With the current scarcity of Schultz books, it is understandable that his readership popularity has waned — a popularity that between the World Wars amounted almost to a cult. *My Life as an Indian* continued to appear in edition after edition, some in condensed form, even in Braille. While no record was kept of the numbers of Schultz books sold here and abroad, the figure has been estimated at upward of two million. Even a recent popularity survey, conducted nearly forty years after Schultz's death among Montana readers of books by Montana authors, disclosed that the list was headed by *My Life as an Indian*.

Schultz' popularity is still a factor to be reckoned with. Four anthologies of his stories have been issued since his death in 1947, two within the last decade. An organization of Schultz enthusiasts called the James Willard Schultz Society has members throughout the country, a quarterly publication, and holds national conventions triennially. They arrange the publication or republication of Schultz books that are otherwise available, if at all, only in shops of rare book dealers.

James Willard Schultz was an unusual boy, and became an unusual man — unorthodox as well as individualistic. He was something of a rebel from the time he was little "Willie Shultz," as it was then spelled in the sleepy little town in upstate New York where he was born to well-to-do parents shortly before the Civil War. His teachers in Sunday and public schools found him difficult, and he failed to finish at a military school where he was sent to prepare for West Point. He never went to college.

Young Schultz's distaste for the humdrum and yearning for adventure swept him into the northwest where wild Indians and hordes of buffalo still roamed. Though not yet 18, on the second day after he arrived at Fort Benton, Montana, in 1877, he was living in a tepee, a Blackfeet lodge. Before he was 21, he married a 15-year-old Piegan girl, and was participating fully in all of the Indian modes of life. He even joined his new friends in inter-tribal warfare.

Although young Schultz's formal education was limited, and he spent much of his early Montana years in isolated Indian trading posts, his inclination to put his thoughts about his new-found people and surroundings into writing surfaced early. He subscribed to two or three eastern periodicals, of which his favorite was a weekly publication in newspaper format called *Forest and Stream*.

Before Schultz had been in Montana three years, he submitted to *Forest and Stream* an article entitled "Hunting in Montana," which referred in passing to his intention to visit Chief Mountain and the St. Mary lakes. This article (see page 1) was published in 1880. By the time he was 23, Schultz had submitted four more pieces to the same publication, all of which were promptly printed. In 1883, at the age of 24, he submitted a series of nine articles entitled "Life Among the Blackfeet." They were published in consecutive issues.

Following these early efforts, Schultz continued to write for *Forest and Stream*, including stories and articles about his guiding trips to the St. Mary country. The most pretentious was a series describing a trip down the Missouri, which was later published as a book, *Floating on the Missouri*.

After he fled Montana in 1904 to escape arrest on a poaching charge, Schultz's activities broadened. He spent time in Arizona, and finally made his headquarters in southern California. Because the recent death of his Indian wife weighed heavily on his mind, he wrote his first book, *My Life as an Indian*. The title suggests an autobiography, but it was in fact a romantic novel centered upon his wife and their life together.

With the success that attended this book, he was able to become a full-time writer, and became acquainted with many of the writers then living in southern California. Schultz interested himself in various causes of the American Indian; and eventually organized and led the fight to persuade Congress to grant full citizenship to the Indian. As time went on, these activities, plus his 40 popular books, and his explorations in the Swiftcurrent and St. Mary areas inspired his reputation as Montana's Renaissance man.

Our paths crossed in the years 1918 and 1920, when we spent summers in Glacier Park, I as a Park employee, he as a guest of the Great Northern. His book *Blackfeet Tales of Glacier National Park* greatly increased interest in the park. Many years later, while preparing a Schultz biography, I learned that he had done some earlier writing which was said to have appeared in the columns of *Forest and Stream*.

I determined to rediscover this pre-1900 Schultz material; to hope that somewhere there might be a complete file of *Forest and Stream*. I assumed it would be in the Library of Congress, but learned that the library did not have a complete set of *Forest and Stream* in microfilm for the period 1880-1894. But, I learned that the library of the University of Montana does have a complete set.

It would be necessary to peruse more than 750 microfilmed issues of *Forest and Stream*, checking 52 editions a year for 15 years. Since each issue had sixteen pages, each with six colums, or 96 columns per issue, the total approximately 750,000 columns, it was a tiresome job, complicated by the absence of a table of contents or index.

The result of that intensive search, which took several weeks, was the articles and stories that make up this book, plus one additional article. That 23rd article is "My First Visit to the St. Mary Lakes." Although not written in the nineteenth century, it has been inserted in this collection of articles and stories covering the 1880-1894 period of Schultz's life for the sake of maintaining chronological continuity. It actually appeared in the *Great Falls Tribune* for November, 1936; but its inclusion enables the reader to absorb the story of Schultz's first visit to the St. Mary country in 1883 before reading the next article covering his 1884 visit to the same area.

It will be noted that the date on the article entitled "To Chief Mountain" is January, 1885, although *Forest and Stream* did not publish it until November, 1885. For some reason, the publication's editor, George Bird Grinnell, although evidently intrigued by Schultz's January, 1885 story, simply failed to publish it until the following November. It appeared one week before Grinnell began his own series of articles on his visit to the same area in September, 1885.

Schultz met George Bird Grinnell in the fall of 1885, when Schultz guided Grinnell's first visit to the St. Mary and Swiftcurrent region of what is now Glacier National Park. During later visits to the same region, they discovered and explored the two largest glaciers in Montana.

Grinnell had been impressed by Schultz's series of sketches entitled "Life Among the Blackfeet," which appeared in *Forest and Stream* in 1883-84. In 1891, when Grinnell was considering preparation of his book *Blackfoot Lodge Tales*, he realized that Schultz had already covered much of his subject. Schultz declined Grinnell's urging that he expand his sketches into a book and offered Grinnell the use of his material and any additional help that he could provide.

Grinnell did make use of some of Schultz's material, notably in the fourth section of *Blackfoot Lodge Tales* entitled "The Story of the Three Tribes." That section dealt with such subjects as the daily life and customs of the Blackfeet, their social organization, religion, and medicine pipes and healing. His borrowing from Schultz is apparent throughout, although not often in identical wording. However, his description of the gentes of the three tribes (see pages 208-210 of *Blackfoot Lodge Tales*), of the punishment for adultery (page 220), and of the "piskans" (pages 230-234) followed Schultz closely. At pages 279-281, Grinnell set forth a long excerpt from Schultz (see pages 77-80 herein), describing in detail the ceremony of the unwrapping of a sacred medicine pipe for the benefit of a sick woman.

Those familiar with Schultz's literary career are aware that it got a late start. Until he left Montana in 1903 or 1904, he had made his living as an Indian trader, as a rancher on the Blackfoot Reservation, and as a mountain guide, apparently giving no thought to writing as a profession. He was nearly 50 when his first book was published in 1907, and did not take up full-time writing until about 1912. He went into high gear in the next 25 years, writing scores of magazine stories, and more than 35 books, using only one publisher, Houghton-Mifflin.

Authors who achieve success usually do so by writing about subjects with which they are most familiar. Schultz was no exception. He had a wide range of experience during his early life and spent the rest of his years writing about it, hence his writing became as diversified as his experience. He had been brought into close contact with the western frontier, from shooting buffalo to working at several Indian trading posts; from marrying an Indian girl to becoming fluent in the difficult Blackfoot language; from ranching for many years on an Indian Reservation to acting as a guide and explorer in parts of the future Glacier National Park; and from working on an archaeological "dig" to acting as a literary editor on a metropolitan daily.

Schultz's work may be roughly divided into three categories: (1) His many tales of western adventure, most of which, despite some factual content, were really fiction, designed to entertain, rather than inform; (2) His biographical and semi-autobiographical books, included *My Life as an Indian, Friends of My Life as an Indian*, and reports of his experiences as a guide and explorer; and (3) His work dealing with the customs and traditions of the Blackfeet that was intended to be entirely non-fiction.

Schultz's work in the latter category was done during his early years in Montana. His "Sketches of Life Among the Blackfeet" were written in 1883, at the age of 24, and without benefit of formal schooling beyond the eleventh grade. That was a year when Joe Kipp had left him in sole charge of the post at Fort Conrad, and during which he made his first visit to the St. Mary region in what is now Glacier National Park.

These sketches were praisd by George Bird Grinnell, an able ethnologist, and by others. In speaking of them, Grinnell wrote (see page xvi of the Introduction to his *Blackfoot Lodge Tales*): "It is most unusual to find anyone living the rough life beyond the frontier, and mingling in daily intercourse with Indians, who has the intelligence to study their traditions, history and customs, and the industry to reduce his observations to writing."

The explanation of this phenomenal accomplishment has to be that he was self-educated. In addition to possessing a high degree of native intelligence, Schultz read voraciously everything on which he could lay hands. We know that he was a subscriber to *Forest and Stream*, and that he quoted articles in *Popular Science Monthly* and from *Century Magazine* (see page 59). From *My Life as an Indian* (page 4), we learn that Schultz had read and re-read Lewis and Clark's *Journal*, Catlin's *Eight Years*, and *The Oregon Trail*. Undoubtedly, he had access to other books, since he wrote learnedly (page 61) concerning the "Mythologic Philosophy of the Blackfeet," alluding to the work of an ethnologist, Major J. M. Powell.

The reader should keep in mind that the articles in this book were written sporadically, whenever the author had the time and the inclination, at a time when Schultz had no idea of becoming a full-time writer. Its contents are varied: a few stories, a few autobiographical articles, his sketches on the Blackfeet — all dealing with the subjects that happened to interest him at the time. Some were later to prove popular with various segments of the reading public.

These early years were a period of growth and development, as well as of the accumulation of much of the material of which Schultz was able to make good use later. Yet the fact that this collection of writing contains one of his most important pieces of work is alone sufficient to warrant publication of the entire collection.

Those who are already familiar with the life of James Willard Schultz may find the contents of this book a welcome addition to their fund of knowledge. For those unacquainted with his career, these few words will provide useful information on his literary career and the popularity he enjoyed during his lifetime.

Warren L. Hanna
1986

Birthplace of Schultz in Booneville, New York.

—Courtesy of Archives, Montana State University Libraries

James Willard Schultz (Apikuni) as a young man in Montana.
—Courtesy of Archives, Montana State University Libraries

Hunting in Montana

A chill, sad ending of a dreary day,
The waning light in stillness dies away;
Bequeaths no ray of hope the void to fill,
But lends to gloomy thoughts more sadness still.

Such were my thoughts as I crouched among the reeds and rushes of a little slough, one day last March [1880]. It was cold, cloudy; and I had been there all day watching for water-fowl with little success, as my bag up to that time was only two geese and five mallards. As I repeated the lines to myself I was preparing to return home, when I heard the familiar and pulse-quickening "Honk! honk!" of a flock of geese, and presently saw them coming straight toward the slough. I did not allow them to light, but just as they were about to, I let both barrels of my No. 10 Webley into them, and dropped three. Before I had time to gather them up, along came some mallards, and I got five of those. Then came a tremendous large flock of little teal, and changing my coarse shot for a couple of charges of No. 8, I dropped nine of them. Then a flock of geese, brant and mallards charged at me, and were repulsed with a loss of four of their number. In fact, I was kept busy loading and firing till dark, my last bird being a fine large swan, which I dropped with a charge of BB. So my day's sport ended finely after all, and next morning I sent the wagon up for the game, and found I had killed thirteen geese, eight brant, seventeen mallards, thirteen teals, five ducks, which I do not know the name of, and one swan, making a total of fifty-seven head, which I call a pretty large bag for two and one-half or three hours shooting.

But waterfowl is not the only game here by any means. Antelope can be seen any day by riding three or four miles from the house.[1] At this time of the year they are not banded together in large numbers as they are in the fall and winter, and are exceedingly hard to approach. I was scouring about on the prairie the other day with an Indian, and we ran over a little band as we turned the point of a ridge. The Indian jumped off his horse and killed four before they could get out of range of his Winchester. I never cared to hunt antelope— in fact, could never find any sport in it; and to me the meat has a strong, disagreeable taste.

Alas! the skeletons which cover the prairie are all we have left to remind us that thousands of buffalo used to roam about here. But I am happy to say that I have killed a few of them before they become extinct. This winter I was over in the Judith Basin for several months with the notorious Indian trader Joe Kipp, who was trading for robes and peltrees with the different tribes of the Blackfoot Nation-Piegans, Bloods and Blackfeet. The average cost of a good robe was about $1.75 and as he traded for about 2,000 robes, he will clear between six and seven thousand dollars.

The timbered bottoms of the river—the Marias—are full of white-tail deer, and the "cooleys," which run out in the prairie, shelter a fair sprinkling of black-tail, sometimes called mule deer. It is with the former, however, that I have the most sport. I have a old Indian mare which I ride when hunting them, and I am sure she enjoys the sport as much as I do, for she will poke along the brush, keeping a sharp lookout, and when she sees one she will stop of her own accord. I remember one day I was hunting with her in the bottom below here, and when passing through the little thicket of cherry and bullberry brush, she stopped all of a sudden, and although I pressed my spur against her side she would not move an inch. Well, I looked and looked, and saw nothing, and was about to give the old beast a good spurring, thinking she had fooled me, when about thirty feet to my left

---

[1]At this time he was living at Fort Conrad.

I saw a little fawn standing staring at me. I immediately gave it my compliments in the shape of nine large buckshot. Another time I scared up a doe and two fawns, dropping the doe and one fawn with a right and left, while the other ran off a little way and stopped. Slipping off my horse, I crept up within range, and killed him also, making three deer in about as many minutes. I always use a shotgun to hunt them, and seldom fail to get a close, fair shot, although I often miss; but, like all hunters, I do not care to tell about the misses.

Of all foolish animals that walk on four feet I think the black-tail deer the most foolish; unless the wind is in their favor, a person can nearly walk over them. I have often heard men telling of standing in one place and killing a whole band. In fact, when we were, "out to buffalo" last winter I saw an Indian clean up a band of seven, shooting from one position. They prefer to stay in a broken, hilly country, where are great high-cut banks and deep cooleys. There is such a place about five miles from here, and I often go out there for a little sport. I killed a buck there one day which I think would have weighed, dressed, over 225 pounds. He had a very large pair of antlers, but, like all black-tail, they were irregular and devoid of beauty.

About thirty miles from here, looming up in all their grandeur, are the snow-capped peaks of the Rocky Mountains. There can be found, mingling with one another, every species of game there is on the North American continent—Mountain buffalo, moose, elk, deer, bighorn and Rocky Mountain sheep; grizzly, cinnamon and black bear; panthers, wolves, lynx, swans, geese, brant, ducks, prairie chickens, grouse, etc., enough to satisfy the wildest dreams of any sportsman.

Then the streams are full of trout, and the larger and deeper lakes have plenty of salmon in them, especially St. Mary's Lake, where it is said salmon have been caught weighing fifty pounds. After the rainy season I intend going up to Chief Mountain and St. Mary's Lake on a hunting expedition. As it is impossible to get among the game with a wagon I shall take an Indian along named *Enucki-yu*[1] He is an A No. 1 Indian; has a large new lodge, plenty of horses to pack the plunder; and last, but not least, three strong women to do all the work. The expense of the trip would be nothing, and good saddle horses can be bought for $20.

The buffalo were about thirty miles from the Post, and as I had no other way of going I accompanied a camp of Piegans; ate like an Indian, slept like an Indian, and found it not very bad living after all. I had heard a great many stories about running buffalo, how dangerous it was, etc., etc.; but when we had arrived on the ground, and one fine morning started out for a run, immediately I saw the buffalo I forgot all about the danger, and was as eager as any one to be in the lead. Seeing a little band running off to the right I let the impatient horse go, and was soon pumping cartridges into them with my Winchester carbine as fast as possible, and at the end of the run found I had slain seven. But instead of shooting choice cows like the Indians, my buffalo were of nearly every age and sex. What dancing and feasting there was in camp that night! The amount of liver and entrails there was roasted and eaten was astonishing and it was kept up every night till we started back to the Judith.

The Indians and whites in this country were all armed with the Winchester gun, the Indians mostly using the '66 model carbine and the whites the '66 and '73 model rifle. Any other kind of gun is seldom seen, there being no sale for them in the country. An attempt was made in Fort Benton last summer to introduce the Burgess gun, but three or four of them burst, and one man had his arm shattered and to-day they could not be given away.

In your issue of March 11 I notice an article on the "Unfrequented Regions of the Adirondacks," by Albert Cornish, in which he says: "The first week I was there I heard a catamount scream regularly every morning at 3 o'clock." Now I would like very much to know what kind of a noise the animal made. I spent nearly the entire winter of '77 and '78

---

[1]Meaning *Little Bear* in Blackfoot.

4

in Brown's Tract, Hamilton and Herkimer counties, N.Y.—which, by the way, has more unfrequented lakes and more game than any other part of the Adirondacks— hunting these very animals with fair success, killing three full grown ones, the largest of which measured over eight feet in length. My companions were Mr. Jack Sheppard and Ed. Arnold, whom all your readers know who have visited Brown's Tract.

These men, Sheppard and Arnold, have been panther hunters from boyhood, and their scores of killed will each reach pretty near a hundred. They solemnly assert that in their whole experience with the "varmits" they have never heard them scream or make any noise whatever unless they were wounded, and by experience I can affirm that when the latter is the case they can *growl* fierce enough to cause a person to lose his hat, lock his snow shoes together, and fall over in entire disregard of a cocked rifle which but a second before, he was pointing at the beast. Yes, I am very anxious to hear what kind of a noise the animal made, and if Mr. Cornish will enlighten us he will greatly oblige.

AP-WA-CUN-NA[1]
Upper Maria's River, Montana Territory

---

[1]It will be noted that Schultz's first five articles or stories are successively signed *Ap-wa-cun-na, Ap-we-cun-ny, Ap-pe-cun-ny, Ap-pe-cun-ny* and *Ap-pe-kun-ny*, indicating uncertainty by Schultz as to how the name should be spelled in English.

The White Buffalo Cow

"*Ap-we-cun-ny*,"[1] said *Pe-nuk-wi-um* to me one evening when we were camped near Black Butte "the young men say that there is a white cow in the band of buffalo below here." A white cow! The words sent an electric thrill all through me, and I unconsciously passed my hand along the barrel of the carbine which lay close by my side. A white cow! One of those rare albinos, so rare that among thousands upon thousands of buffalo I had never seen one of them. For a long time I had hoped to come across one of these animals, but as time passed and the buffalo kept decreasing in number, I finally concluded it would never be my lot to chase one of them. Here was a chance. A white cow was close by, and I determined to kill it or kill my horse in pursuit.

"*Pe-nuk-wi-um*," I said, "let us 'make medicine,' and you tell the sun I want to kill that white cow."

"Ah, that will be good," he replied, and accordingly unwrapped the sacred "medicine pipe," filled and lighted it and blowing a few whiffs toward the sky and the ground, repeated the following prayer:

> "Oh Sun. Oh, World-maker. Take pity. Not far off a white cow stops; it is with many buffalo. Take pity. We are not strong. You are strong. Long ago you went behind the mountains. Be quick and get up early tomorrow morning. One white man stops here. His name

---

[1]At the time this article was written, Schultz was spelling his Blackfoot name *Ap-we-cunny*, not *Ap-pe-cunny*. See spelling of signature on page 10.

is *Ap-we-cun-ny*. Take pity. Give him *Nat-o-yi* (that of the sun). Give his horse *Nat-o-yi*, so he can kill the white cow. We will not eat it. We will tan the robe and hang it in a tree. The robe we will give to you. I have said."

As he concluded and passed me the long pipe I asked him why we would not eat the meat of the white cow. "Because," he replied, "because the sun owns the white cow. He sends it from way off in the sky. It is his and we must not eat it. We must give him the robe. We must tan it soft and white and hang it up where he can see it. Then he is glad."

Taking down a yellow and red painted "medicine sack," which hung over his head, *Pe-nuk-wi-um* emptied its contents into his lap—queer stones, little fossilized snails, etc. Singling out one perfectly round pebble he gave it to me, saying, "Keep it. I give it to you. It is the sun's, and we call it a buffalo rock. When you wear it your horse will not fall; you will shoot straight; you will kill the white cow."

Of course during all this I kept a perfectly grave face. For it is only by seeming to believe that a person can get an Indian to talk on these subjects. I had been so successful with *Pe-nuk-wi-um* that he thought I believed in his religion and legends as much as any one of his tribe.

"Well, *Pe-nuk-wi-um*," I said, after a long silence, "tell me one short story and then we will go to bed."

"All right," he replied; "I will tell you a short one about the Old Man (Old Man: a mythical person who forms the chief subject of Blackfoot legends).

> Once the Old Man was taking a walk. It was night, but the moon and stars were all looking down, so it was not very dark. When crossing a little prairie he heard music, which seemed to come from a hole in the ground. 'Ha! Who can be in there, I wonder,' said the Old Man to himself, and looking in he saw a multitude of mice having a war-dance, some of them beating drums and others dancing about the fire singing and brandishing spears of grass over their heads. 'I would like to dance with you,' said the Old Man. 'Come in, come in,' replied

the Mice. 'Poke your head one way and another and the hole will be large enough.' When the Old Man got inside the Chief mouse said, 'Let's have plenty of fun—let's dance all night, and the first one who gets sleepy is to have his hair cut off.' 'Good, good!' all exclaimed, and then the dance commenced, each one trying to dance the best. When it was almost morning the Old Man said, 'Now all of you sit down and drum, and I will show you a new kind of dance.' The Old Man soon became interested in his dance and forgot all about the music till he was tired; then looking up, he saw all the Mice sitting in their places fast asleep, their heads nodding like spears of grass in the wind. 'Ha! ha! You are all asleep, are you?' he said, and taking out his knife he went around and cut off all of their whiskers, singing:

'Ki-nus-ke-ni-yah.
I-wah-pe-noak-si.
Oak-se-est-ce-yah.
Muck-stoak-ce-est-yah.'

"Pipe is out, *Ap-we-cun-ny*," said *Pe-nuk-wi-um*, as he knocked the ashes out of the great red-stone bowl we had been smoking; and we turned in.

Next morning we were up quite early. Too excited to eat a regular breakfast, I swallowed a few mouthfuls of boiled buffalo ribs while cleaning out my Winchester carbine and filling my cartridge belt. Then I examined the cincha and sewing of my "running saddle," made of buckskin filled with antelope hair and devoid of stirrups—a buffalo runner wanting no such death-traps to entangle him in case of a fall. Soon the horses were driven in, and singling out my favorite I bid the woman saddle it. "Saddle a horse for me," said *Pe-nuk-wi-um* to his women. "Yes, saddle a buffalo horse for *Pe-nuk-wi-um*, he is going to kill the white cow," I remarked. At this there was a general laugh, for *Pe-nuk-wi-um* is so heavy that the best horse in camp could not carry him and run a hundred yards. "No, no," he replied. "I am only going to the top of the hill where I can see *Ap-we-cun-ny* shoot the white cow." By the time we were mounted all the rest were ready, and together we started out toward the herd. Some three hundred men were to run that day, many of them as determined to kill the white cow as myself. When they saw me they looked disappointed. "Are you going to run?" said one to me. "No," I replied. "I am afraid to run after the white cow." At this they brightened up considerably, and in less than five minutes the whole party understood that *Ap-we-cun-ny*, who had the fastest horse in camp, was only going to look on. *Pe-nuk-wi-um*, riding by my side laughed, and quietly remarked that my horse might run away with me.

After half a hour's easy ride we came in sight of the buffalo, which were feeding on the edge of a high level prairie. A convenient "coulie" ran along close to them, and entering it, we carefully approached the band. Arriving within a hundred yards of them, we slowly climbed the hill, and then the horses, catching sight of the buffalo made a simultaneous rush at them. Soon the firing commenced, many of the Indians having no hopes of catching the white cow and starting in at the outset to make a big killing. Way up at the head of the band we could see the animal, and, with about two hundred others, I started after it. Our horses seemed to fly over the ground. An occasional bull, coming too close, was dropped to clear the way. Past hundreds of shaggy, sharp horned animals we rode, every nerve strained, and our hearts, seemingly in our throats, beating time to the thunder of a thousand hoofs. In the excitement we jumped ditches and mudholes which in calmer moments we would never have attempted, but would have preferred to go several miles around. But no one thought of the danger. Several horses fell throwing their riders far over their heads. No one looked back to see if they were hurt. We were not within three hundred yards of the white cow. It was time to make a dash, and hitting my horse several times with a heavy rawhide *quirt*, I soon left all my competitors behind. But I found that the white cow was no easy animal to catch. It seemed to know that I was close in pursuit, and left the band in order to run faster. For a time I despaired of getting close enough to shoot; but my horse, perceiving what I was after, redoubled his energies, and before long I was within easy range. Bang! The cow dropped, and as quickly rose and ran. Bang! She dropped again and arose, but this time stood still. Bang again! She dropped, and with a quivering, rattling gasp, expired. Dismounting, I unsaddled the horse to roll and rest. Then I inspected the cow, which I found to be like any other buffalo, with the exception of light, dirty cream-colored hair; but it was a *white cow*, and I had added another feature to my cap. After a time *Pe-nuk-wi-um*'s women came up, and giving them charge of the animal, I resaddled my horse and slowly rode back to camp. The news had already arrived there, and I found the lodge full of men, waiting to hear the details of the run. *Pe-nuk-wi-um* was holding forth, talking excitedly. "Last night," he said, "we made medicine. I asked the sun to give *Ap-we-cun-ny* the white cow. I gave him a buffalo rock, and he wore it in his shirt. Is it not so, *Ap-we-cun-ny*?"

"Ah," I answered, "it is the truth. I knew I was going to kill the white cow. I heard a voice right over the lodge before I got up. It said, 'The white cow is *Ap-we-cun-ny*'s—the white cow is *Ap-we-cun-ny*'s.'"

"Ah." said *Ph-nuk-wi-um*,[1] "I heard it too."

"Hi, hi, hi-i-i!" muttered the listeners. *"Skoon-i-taps Nat-o-yi, Ap-we-cun-ny"*—Strong sun power Ap-we-cun-ny's.

---

[1]Actual spelling used by Schultz in this story. It should have been *Pe-nuk-wi-um*. It means Seen From Afar.

Ap-we-cun-ny
Upper Marias River, M. T.

An Elk Hunt by Moonlight

While hunting among the Rockies in the vicinity of Chief Mountain, several summers ago, I came upon a little glade one day which held in its centre a miniature pond. Around its shores the elk had trod the grass with their sharp hoofs until very little verdure remained. Two well-worn trails led off up the mountain, and all the signs indicated that this was an every-day—or night—watering place for these animals. At the time I found it the sun was nearly set and I had to hurry in order to reach camp before dark. So taking a hasty survey of the place, with many a wistful glance at the track of some monster elk, I hastily descended the canyon and reached camp none too soon, as the gathering darkness was accompanied by a violent thunder storm, which "turned loose" just as I entered the lodge.

It commenced with a low muttering of thunder and occasional vivid flashes of lightning, which illumined far-away precipices and lofty peaks with startling distinctness. The very seams of a distant ledge and the fibrous roots of a stunted pine were revealed by an unusually bright flash. Shortly the thunder became louder and nearer and seemed to batter and crash up against the rocky cliffs in successive charges, as if Nature had brought out all her artillery to rend the very mountains. Then came the hail—great pearl-like balls of ice—which rattled down upon the lodge and through the smokehole with chilling effect, several times subduing the few embers which fitfully flickered in the fire-place.

Perhaps nothing so lowers a man's estimate of his power and importance as a thunder-storm. Then, as crash after crash sounds over his head and the lightning seems to play about his very feet, he realizes his littleness—his utter insignificance. Among such mighty contending elements he realizes that he is of no more consequence than a leaf blown about by the fitful wind.

The storm quickly passed over and finally died away in the distance. With long-drawn breath of relief and a murmured "Thank God," I started to build up the fire. As I did so *Pe-nuk-wi-um* and his family emerged from under sundry heaps of bedding and robes, which were piled promiscuously in different parts of the lodge. They looked so ridiculous as they crawled forth that I couldn't help but smile and finally burst out in a loud ha, ha, ha!

"Do not laugh, my friend," said the chief, solemnly, "do not laugh. The thunder and lightning are great chiefs. Do not laugh—they might come back and kill us."

If a war party of Sioux had suddenly come upon us I do not think *Pe-nuk-wi-um* and his family could have been more frightened. They sat huddled about the fire and in trembling tones recounted the disasters they had known to be caused by the dread elements.

To change the subject, I told the chief about the lakelet I had discovered.

"Ah, I know the place well," he said. "When a young man I killed many elk down there. The elk come there only in the night to drink, and when the night was day (moonlight) we used to go there to kill them. We would hide in the bushes by the trails. We would hide so good that even the birds could not see us from all animals. Far off we could hear the elk coming down the trail. They would often stop to bite off a mouthful of green leaves; then they would come a little closer and stop to look. 'Ah, smart elk!' I used to say to myself, 'I see you, but you can't see me. Come closer, I want to see if your heart is good.' Then they would come nearer and the chief elk would stop right in front of me. Then my arm was strong. I drew the arrow back, took a careful aim and shot right where the moon shone bright on his side. Buzz! the arrow went right into his heart and he lay down. Then I shot fast. All my arrows lay on the ground before me and I kept shooting till the band ran away."

"It is moonlight now, *Pe-nuk-wi-um*," said I; "let's go up there to-morrow night?"

"Ah, I am not a young man any more," he replied. "The winters sit on my head and make a heavy load to carry. My legs are not strong any more."

"But it isn't far," I said.

"Well," he answered, "I will go with you, but we will have to travel slowly; there are many rocks to go over, and I cannot jump them like the sheep."

The next afternoon, after two or three hours of slow walking and climbing, we arrived at the little lakelet. I noticed with satisfaction that quite a number of elk had visited the place during the night. In several places where I had walked about in the mud the day before I found that they had obliterated nearly all traces of footprints. It was yet an hour or more till dark, and to pass away the time we sat down on a fallen log to smoke and chat. From our elevated position we had a spendid view of the country to the East. About eighty miles distant the three lonely buttes of the Sweet Grass hills stood surrounded by a sea of prairie, and still further eastward the blue outlines of the Bear's Paw mountains loomed up against the sky. Southeast, far beyond the Missouri, I recognized several of the Moccasin and Snowy mountains, over which I had clambered in pursuit of mountain sheep.

As the sun gradually sunk in the West, we ate our lunch of boiled meat, bread and dried bull-berries. The bull-berry (called by the Blackfeet, *Mic-sin-it-sim*) forms one of their principal articles of diet, and is gathered in huge quantities by the squaws, who cut off the bushes and beat them over blankets with sticks. In color and taste this berry resembles the red currant, and is, perhaps, a trifle more tart in flavor.

"*Appe-cun-ny*," said *Pe-nuk-wi-um*, suddenly, "did you

ever hear about the Old Man and the bull-berries?"

"No!"

"Then I will tell you the story."

"Once the Old Man was walking by the river, when he thought he saw some nice large berries in the water, and taking off his clothes jumped in after them. When he got in the water, however, he could not find the berries, and climbing out on the bank was about to put on his clothes, when looking down in the water he again saw the berries, and once more jumped in after them. This operation he repeated a number of times, until he finally became enraged, and tearing up his robe bound some stones to his feet with the strips, determined to jump far enough and deep enough to get the berries. But he was too strong, and jumped way out where the water was black and deep. Down, down he went, and nearly drowned. He finally succeeded though in breaking the strips which held the stones to his legs, and, tired and half strangled, climbed out on the bank to rest. As he lay there he happened to look up overhead and saw great bunches of berries growing on the bushes, and immediately perceived how he had been fooled by the reflection of them in the water. Picking up a club he threw it at them, saying, 'There, I will make thorns grow on you, and after this any one who wants to gather you will have to knock you off with clubs.'"

And now the sun had set, and we repaired to the places we had picked out to watch the trails. *Pe-nuk-wi-um* taking the left one and I the right.

My hiding place was not more than fifty feet from the trail, and commanded a long reach of the path where the sun shone brightly through the stunted pines. As the slight wind was blowing down the mountain in the direction from which the elk would come, I dared to light my pipe, and sat for a long time thinking of bygone exploits of mountain and prairie. Hoo, hoo, hoo, hoo hoo! cried an owl way up on the mountain side, and from the dark recesses below its mate answered back in a repetition of hoots. What hunter but loves to hear the hoot of the owl! What pleasant memories has he of bygone sport, of peaceful camping in the woods, of silent paddling among the lily pads where the mist winds fantastically upward, but what are associated with the melancholy notes of this queerest of queer birds.

In my wanderings among the mountains and prairies I miss one old friend of Eastern days—the loon! How many nights have I lain awake in the depths of some Eastern forest and listened to its weird, long-drawn cry arise from the lake, and, echoing from hill to hill, finally die away in the distance. But, hark! No more dreaming. I heard something surely! Yes, I hear it again, the tread of some heavy animal coming down *Pe-nuk-wi-um*'s trail. A bright flash from the chief's gun, a report, followed by a moment's silence. Then from the animal the most unearthly, hideous yell ever heard. I recognized it. *Pe-nuk-wi-um* had wounded a grizzly! Perhaps there were more with it! Perhaps—but I waited no longer. I heard something coming through the bushes toward me, and turning, fled with all speed down the mountain. As I crossed the glade I saw the chief emerge from his hiding-place, in spite of his weight and years running like a deer. He was soon beside me, and together we kept on down the mountain. Over rocks and logs, jumping deep holes, we kept on and on, never stopping till we reached the prairie. Exhausted and faint, we sank down upon the grass and tried to regain our breath.

"What was it?" I asked. "A bear," gasped the chief.

"Did you kill it?" "I don't know," he replied. "I saw its eyes in the bushes and thought it was an elk. I fired, it yelled, and I ran away as quick as I could." No more hunting that night. So we quietly wended our way back to camp and to bed, but it was long before we fell asleep. Never in my life had I received such a scare. That terrifying yell still echoed in my ears and my heart beat faster every time I thought of it.

Well, of course, by breakfast time the whole camp had heard of our exploit, and many were the questions asked and tales recounted about the bear. Accompanied by six or eight young men, I went back to the lakelet. Arriving there, we deployed and slowly reconnoitered the ground. Step by step we advanced to the thicket where *Pe-nuk-wi-um* had seen the bear. Not a sound was heard. "I guess it's dead," said one. "I don't believe he killed it," said another. "Look," said another, and running a little distance held up a dead lynx to view. "Hi-hi-hi" they all shouted. "Look at *Pe-nuk-wi-um*'s and *Ap-pe-cun-ny*'s bear. See the big bear which yelled. See the big bear which chases them down the mountain." There was no doubt about it. To *Pe-nuk-wi-um*'s distorted vision the lynx had seemed an elk and a bear, and my ears had willingly deceived me as to the cry. Carefully strapped to a pole, the animal was triumphantly borne into camp and received with shouts of derision by the people.

Poor *Pe-nuk-wi-um*! He never heard the end of the elk hunt. Many a time since have I heard the Indians, speaking of the lynx, call it "Pe-nuk-wi-um's elk."

Ap-pe-cun-ny
Fort Benton, M. T., April 25, 1881

The *Pis-Kan* of the Blackfeet

The Blackfeet Indians, and perhaps many others, have a peculiar habit of going up on high hills and bluffs conveniently close to camp and sitting there motionless and rigid as statues for hours. Near the close of the day seems to be the particular time for indulging in this practice. Why they do so is a mystery. I have often asked them the reason, and have invariably received the reply, *Kis-tohts*, meaning "for nothing." Sometimes I have hidden myself in the coarse rye grass which grows so tall and luxuriantly in the river bottoms, and with the aid of a powerful field glass have closely scrutinized their countenances, but to no purpose. The expression of their faces never changed. Their eyes had a far-off dreamy look which could not be interpreted. Perhaps, as they look over the broad, almost limitless prairies, nowadays so seldom dotted with the dark forms of the buffalo and the graceful bands of antelope pleasant memories of boyhood days come crowding up in their minds. More likely, however, as they gaze over the great rolling prairie, at the blue mountains looming up so grandly in the distance, and at the broad timbered valley of the river so long the homes of their ancestors, their hearts are sad to think how everything is changing; how in a short time the buffalo shall have passed away; and how where the rich bunch grass used to grow the white man will plant strange weeds and roots. No wonder that their hearts are sad and that their prayers against the whites are bitter.

Unperceived I once heard an old man thus address his medicine or "secret helper." He said:

I-yu Ksis-tuk-ki, Ke-nuk-o-qui-tup-pi.
Listen, Beaver, so I can get something.

Kim-at-o-kit! Kim-at-o-kit! un-is-tuh-kuh so-ohts-oh pek-se at-se-mo-ye-kah-quo-to-mo-kit.
Take pity on me! Take pity on me! That little under the water animal pray for me.

An-si-tis nat-os o-nis-ti nat-os ne-tap-i
Tell him the sun, wonderful sun regularly

pah-kok-sin-e-kah-pah nap-i-quon.[1] (Curse[2]) white man.

The earnestness of the old man as he delivered this prayer, and the intensity of the curse, the most forcible in the Blackfoot language, firmly impressed it upon my memory. Let me here add, for the benefit of those who may be interested in such subjects, that the Blackfeet pray to the Sun, the supreme power, through the medium of their medicine, or in their own language, "secret helpers," which are generally animals.

But when I began this article I intended to tell you how the Blackfeet caught buffalo in ancient days; and I now turn to that subject.

Not so very long ago I happened to be camped with a gens of the *Pe-gun-ny*,[3] at the place called Willows Round, situated some fifteen miles above here, on the Marias River. Early in the evening I saw old *Po-kah-yah-yi*, in whose lodge I was stopping, ascend a steep bluff not far off, and, giving him time to reach the top, I followed and was soon seated by his side. Directly opposite us across the river were the remains of a *pis-kan*, or, as the white men out here call it, a "buffalo pond." Why so called I cannot say, the literal translation of the word *pis-kan* being "falling-off place." "Now my

---

[1] *Nap-i-quot*, not *Nap-i-quon*, as spelled by Schultz.
[2] Cannot be translated. (Schultz footnote).
[3] *Pe-cun-ny*, not *Pe-gun-ny*, as spelled by Schultz.

friend," said I after I had regained my breath, "tell me about that *pis-kan*. How did you make it; how many buffalo did you catch in one day; and how many winters ago did you use it?"

The old man's story was as follows:

"In those days we had no guns, but used to kill many buffalo with bows and arrows; and sometimes, we used the *pis-kan*. When we made a *pis-kan*, we first found a little open glade by the river where the prairies came down and ended in a cut bank as high as a man. From this cut bank we build a strong fence clear around the edge of the glade. We used big trees to make the fence— logs and sticks, and anything that would help to keep the buffalo from breaking out. Then we built two lines of stone piles far out on the prairie, two lines that never diverged from each other. Then the *pis-kan* was built.

"The night before we intended to make a drive we always had a buffalo dance. All the people danced. The medicine men all wore buffalo robes and sung the buffalo songs. Everyone prayed to their secret helpers for good luck. Early the next morning the people went out, and hid behind the stone piles on the prairie. The medicine man who was going to call the buffalo put on a buffalo robe, hair side out, and sitting down smoked one pipe to the Sun. Then he spoke to his wives and all the women of his lodge, saying, 'You must not go outside until I return. You must not look out of the doorway or any hole. Take this sweet grass,' giving it to his head wife, 'and every little while burn a small part of it so that the Sun will be glad. Pray that we will have good luck.' Then he mounted a dark colored horse and rode out on the prairie. When he came near a band of buffalo he began to ride quickly in circles and cried out to the buffalo, saying, *'E-ne-uh! E-ne-uh!'* (meaning "Buffalo!") The buffalo were first a little scared; then they began to follow him slowly; and soon ran after him as fast as they could. Then the medicine man rode into the shoot, and after the buffalo had also run in he jumped out to one side of the stone piles, and the herd passed by. The people behind kept rising up and shouting, which made them run all the faster. The buffalo in the head of the band were afraid of the stone piles, and kept right on in the middle of the shoot; those in the rear were scared by the people continually rising behind them, and so pushed the leaders ahead. When the band had got close to the edge of the *pis-kan*, all the people closed in on them and with a great shout drove them over the cut bank into the enclosure. Then with their bows and arrows, the men killed all the buffalo; even the old bulls were killed. The fattest cows were then marked for the chiefs and medicine men by placing sticks on the tails, and the rest were divided among the people."

The above narrative is true in every respect. As late as 1865 the *Pe-gun-ny*[1] used these *pis-kans* on the Upper Marias. Mr. Jos. Kipp, the well-known Indian trader, tells me that in 1864 he saw the *Pe-gun-ny*[2] capture over seventy-five head of buffalo in this manner. Sometimes three or four drives were made in one day. About seventy-five buffalo were the average drive, though sometimes more than a hundred were taken.

Ap-pe-cun-ny
Upper Marias River, M. T., April 15, 1882

---

[1] *Pe-cun-ny*, not *Pe-gun-ny*, as spelled by Schultz.
[2] Idem.

Old Eagle-Head's Sepulchre

At last after an absence of many months I am back here on the upper Marias.[1] Here I am in the same old room; my guns are again resting on the familiar hooks of dried deer-legs, and my blankets are spread on the same shaky bedstead as of yore. Still I am not happy. My heart is now set on spending the summer in the Rockies, and as I take my field-glass every day and see the great banks of snow covering them nearly to the base, I grow impatient and wonder if the sun isn't losing its power, for although more than a month has elapsed since I first looked at those awful snow banks, I cannot see that they have diminished at all in size. But the river flowing so swiftly by the door says I am mistaken. Its waters are steadily rising, telling of many a liquified snowdrift gliding down to the sea. "Have patience," it calls out with a gurgle as it sweeps around the sharp cut bank and dashes over the ford, and with a sigh half of impatience and half of relief I turn away and busy myself as best I can.

Yesterday I saddled a steady old Indian horse and rode up the "Dry Fork," which by the way hasn't been dry for the last six years. Took both my guns, strapping the Winchester to my saddle and carrying the fowling piece in my hands. After going about a mile I heard the unmistakable sound of a rattlesnake and looked around just in time to see a monster one disappear in its hole. Having nothing better to do I picketed the horse at a distance and then lay down near the hole and waited for the snake to appear. Ere long he poked

---

[1]Fort Conrad

21

his head out and not seeing me, for I was hid behind a bunch of rye grass, he slowly crawled forth and coiled himself up for a comfortable doze in the warm sunshine. I rudely disturbed him with a charge of No. 6 which made him writhe and rattle furiously, blew his head to atoms with the other barrel and started on my way rejoicing.

This Dry Fork is a great resting place for ducks, and I rode along its banks in hope of bagging a few mallards or teal. I am about to make a confession. I fear I cannot class myself as one of the sporting fraternity, as a "true sportsman," for I am a pot-hunter. Back at the fort our meat larder was empty, and had been so for several days. It was with the mercenary object of filling the empty pot that I started out on this day's hunt. I am worse than a pot-hunter. I am a very fiend of destruction! for at this time of year the ducks are nesting, and in every female duck I killed I of course destroyed a prospective brood of ducklings, and a "true sportsman" wouldn't do such a thing as that. A hungry stomach is not conducive to philanthropy, I thought, as I bagged a fine drake mallard, and, a little later, its mate, which was nesting under a bunch of willows. Following up the creek a mile or two further, I killed six more mallards and two teal.

Up here, near the bank of the river, stands a single isolated cottonwood tree, and in it, resting on a nude scaffold, sleeps a long silent member of the Blackfoot Nation. 'Twas long ago on a summer's day (so I am told) that old Eagle-head died, and here ere the sun set his wives and female relatives brought him to sleep his last sleep. From his aerial sepulchre his soul could look out over the pleasant valley, over the broad prairies and at the dim, distant mountains. On warm summer days the buffalo and antelope would come to drink of the clear water running past the roots of the tree. In the still calm night, the fawn, with its mother, would gambol on the green sward below. Over there, on the point of the hill, the wolves would sit and howl as in days of yore. Ah! how pleasant to be buried in the midst of familiar scenes. No cold weight of earth and metal imprisons old Eagle-head. Here he sleeps in sight of the scenes of his youth, and here he shall sleep until, with the coming years, the tree decays and falls to the ground and his dust is lost in the earth.

Although it is ten or twelve years since the old man died, the scaffold and wrappings are in a good state of preservation. I climbed the tree to get a better view. Between two large branches a scaffold had been built of stout large poles, and on it the body had been securely fastened with broad thongs of buffalo hide. The head was pillowed on several medicine bags, the wrappings of robes, blankets and dressed skins had been partially torn by the eagles or hawks and exposed to view the bow and arrows, shield and other implements which the old man is now supposed to be using in the spirit land. I had some thought of taking these weapons, but just then a passing breeze caused the torn skins to flap and flutter, and hastily descending the tree I mounted the horse and rode away.

I am about to give you conclusive evidence that I am a pot-hunter of the deepest dye. A little further up the creek I saw an antelope, picketed the horse and I managed to crawl up within easy range. Saw it was a doe, and knew if I killed it the poor little fawn cached somewhere on the prairie would die; shot her, however, and tied the carcass on the saddle with great satisfaction, and as I thought of the savory stews and roasts the meat would make, returned home with all speed. Verily I am a true pot-hunter, for I seek to fill the pot with meat, and some of you who, on a favorite stand bag a hundred or so of water fowl in a day, or on the seashore mow down long swaths of poor little snipe, or on a hot summer day catch basket after basketful of trout are "true sportsmen," because you hunt, and fish in season and only for sport. And then you wonder why the grouse are decreasing, and why the ducks are not so plenty as they used to be, and lay it all to the pot-hunter. Next fall when you go out on your annual hunts don't try to kill all the grouse in the woods in one day. Don't kill a wagon load of water fowl just because you can. Be satisfied with moderate bags, and in a few years you will see the wisdom thereof. And now, having said enough to be "cussed" by all hands I will close.

Ap-pe-cun-ny

Life Among the Blackfeet

First Paper

From where rise the transparent, rushing streams, which form the headwaters of that mighty northern river, the Saskatchewan, south to the Yellowstone; from the foothills of the Rocky Mountains between these two rivers, east to about the 104th meridian of longitude, west from Greenwich, was once the home of the Blackfeet. Here, as nowhere else in our whole country, has nature piled up great mountains and spread out vast prairies with a more than lavish hand. All along the western border of this region, the Rockies lift their snow-capped peaks above the clouds. In the northwestern part are the Porcupine Hills. Southeast of these the three lonely buttes of the Sweet Grass Hills stand surrounded by a vast expanse of prairie. Further to the southeast, and running parallel with the Missouri are the Bear's Paw and Little Rocky Mountains. South of the Missouri, between it and the Yellowstone, is a vast cluster of ranges, the Highwood, Belt, Judith, Moccasin and Snowy Mountains. Between these mountain ranges, and between the river valleys stretches everywhere the great prairie. Not the brilliantly flowered prairie of the south, nor the green marshy plains of the far north. Except for a few short weeks in early spring, the short, sparse bunch grass is sere and yellow. The ashy gray of the sage brush but adds to the general sombreness of the landscape. Perhaps in the distance a range or two of mountains may loom up with startling distinctness, although a hundred miles away, or they may appear enveloped in a blue misty haze, the "gathering of the ghosts." The seemingly dreary prairie is not without its beauty. Everywhere it is cut and seamed with great deep ravines, whose perpendicular walls are crowned with fantastic columns and figures of sandstone, carved by the storms and winds of age. Here and there, on some high bleak ridge, a few scattering pines may be seen; short stunted trees with huge gnarled limbs and great black roots which twine around rocks and creep into fissures, seeking a secure foothold against the fierce blasts of winter.

Not so very long ago these prairies were graced with countless herds of buffalo and antelope; along the wooded valleys of the stream, and on the pine covered slopes of the mountains, were once numberless bands of elk, deer, sheep and bears. Some of the game is yet to be found. Bands of the ancient inhabitants are yet to be seen—small remnants of a once mighty nation. Still camping where their forefathers were wont to pitch their lodges, some of them preserve their native dignity and hold to their ancestral customs as sacredly as ever; others are demoralized, discouraged and indifferent. On the prairie, but partly concealed by the thin grass, lie the bleached skeletons of the buffalo. In the trees by the river, securely fastened on their aerial sepulchres, lie the motionless forms of the many dead, whose ghosts are happy in another land. The broad, deep trails, where thousands were wont to pass on their annual hunts, are now grass-grown and nearly obliterated by the leveling hand of time. To those who were accustomed to see the prairie covered with living forms, the smoke of a thousand lodges curling upward in the still, clear air, the change is marvellous which a few short years have wrought. There are those of us, idle dreamers, who would that it might be otherwise. But it may not be. The weaker organism must give way to the stronger, the lower to the higher intellect. Before the bullets and far deadlier firewater of the whites, these simple men have been swept away like leaves before a wind. "But they were only Indians," say some. True: yet they were human beings, they loved their wild, free life as well as we love our life; they had pleasures and sorrows as well as we.

It is not the purpose of this paper to give a history of the Blackfeet since the discovery of their country by the whites. It is enough to say that like most all other Indians they have bitterly opposed the march of civilization and have been defeated, and that the "Piegans," one of the tribes of the Blackfeet yet remaining on United States territory, are in as destitute a condition as is possible for a people to be.

According to tradition, the first white men the Blackfeet ever saw were a detachment of the Hudson's Bay Company, which established a trading post on the Saskatchewan at the close of the last century. In the journal of Lewis and Clark's expedition the narrator mentions meeting the Blackfeet when the expedition were on this side of the main range. Blackfoot tradition, however, makes no mention of this fact, and the writer is inclined to believe that some other tribe must have been mistaken for Blackfeet. Surely such an important event as the first visits of the white men to their country would have been included in their traditions, and in their unwritten history. Mr. Jas. Kipp[1] has the honor of being the first white man they ever saw south of the Saskatchewan, he having come up the Missouri to the mouth of the Marias River with an expedition of the American Fur Company's men in 1832.

At the time the American Fur Company established its post at the mouth of the Marias, the Blackfoot nation was in its prime. At that time it is said to have numbered some 2,500 lodges, or 25,000 people.[2] It was the largest and most powerful body of Indians in the Northwest. Together with its allies, the Sarcees and Gros Ventres, some twenty hostile tribes were without difficulty kept beyond the boundaries of its vast hunting ground.

---

[1]Schultz's early history was faulty. He overlooks the fact that Anthony Henday met the Blackfeet in 1754-55. Hugh Monroe lived with them commencing in 1815; and by 1828, Kenneth McKenzie was trading with them at his post at the mouth of the Marias.

[2]This figure is now considered a gross misrepresentation.

The Blackfoot nation consists of three tribes, the Blackfeet, Bloods and Piegans. Each tribe consists of a number of "gentes" a "gens" being a body of consanguineal kindred in the male line. Below is a complete list of the gentes of each tribe. The writer has taken great pains to translate the names so as to retain the meaning as closely as possible. Any one familiar with an Indian language will understand how difficult is to accomplish.

Tribe *Siks-uh-kah*—Blackfoot, from *Siks-i-nuts*, black, and *uh-kuh-tehit*, foot.

GENTES;
Puh-ksi-nah-mah-yiks—Rotten bows.
Mo-tah-tos-iks—Many medicines.
Siks-in-o-kahs—Black elks.
E-ma-ta-pahk-si-yiks—Dogs naked.
Ah-ki-stan-iks—Much manure.
I-yo-mo-ke-kan-iks—Sliders.
Si-yeks—Liars.
I-sik-stuk-iks—Biters.
Pis-ti-kum-iks
Sin-ik-sis-tso-yiks—Early finished eating.
Ap-pe-ki-yiks—Skunks.
Ik-si-sak-wi-ah-wat-op-iks—Meat-eaters.

Tribe "Bloods," *Ki-nah*. The meaning of this word is uncertain. Perhaps it was originally *Ah-ki-nah*—many chiefs.

GENTES;
Siks-in-o-kahs—Black elks.
I-yo-mo-ke-kan-iks—Sliders
Ah-uo-nis-tsests—Many lodge poles.
Ah-tut-o-si-ki-nah—Behind direction "Bloods."
Is-tse-Ke-nah—"Bloods."
In-uhk-so-yis-sum-iks—Long tail lodge pole.
Ne-tit-skihs—One fighters.
Pis-ksis-sti-yiks.
Siks-ah-pun-iks—Black blood.
A-kik-sum-un-iks.
E-sis-o-kas-im-iks—Hair shirts.

Ah-ki-po-kaks—Many children.
Sak-se-nah-mah-yiks—Short bows.
Ap-pe-ki-yiks—Skunks
Ak-o-tash-iks—Many horses.

Tribe "Piegans," *Pe-kun-i*—spotted tan, that is, a robe which has hard spots on it after being tanned.

GENTES;
E-nuk-s-iks—Small.
Ap-pe-ki-yiks—Skunks.
Ke-me-tiks—Buffalo manure.
E-pok-se-miks—Fat roasters.
Ah-pi-tup-iks—Blood people.
Ne-tyu-yiks—One eaters.
Kut-i-im-iks—? Laugh.
Sik-ut-si-pum-iks—Black moccasin soles.
Sin-ik-sis-two-yiks—Early finished eating.
Me-ah-wah-pet-seks—Seldom lonesome.
Mo-twin-iks—All chiefs.
E-nuk-si-kah-ko-pwa-iks.
Isk-sin-i-tup-iks—Worm people.
Me-oh-kiu-i-yeks—Big tops.
Sik-o-pok-si-miks—Black fat roasters.
Mo-kum-iks—Mad campers.
Ne-tot-si-tsis-stum:iks—Bulls come close.
Sik-oh-ket-sim-iks—Black smoke holes.
Mo-tah-tos-iks—Many medicines.
Ne-tak:us-kit-se-pup-iks—One will their hearts.
Ah-ki-ye-ko-kin-iks—Many loose women.

It will readily be seen from the translations of the above, that each gens takes its name from some peculiarity or habit it is supposed to possess. Thus, the Blackfoot gens "sliders" was so named on account of the great love the people had for sliding down the banks into the ice on buffalo ribs. "Behind direction" is the name of the north. The gens "Behind direction" Bloods was so called because it was greatly attached to an extreme northern portion of the great hunting grounds. The gens *Kut-i-im-iks*—? Laugh," was so called because its members were seldom seen to laugh. *Kut-i* is the sound which asks a direct question and may be represented in our language by the words do, did, is, are, and was, when used in asking direct questions. The Piegan gens "Blood-people," received its name on account of its members' abnormal appetite for cooked blood. The name of the gens "Small" is perhaps the only one which gives no clue to its meaning. Long ago, says tradition, this gens was out on a hunting expedition, and, meeting a camp of mountain Indians, traded buffalo robes for robes of different mountain animals. Upon returning to camp the other Piegans were surprised to see them wearing such small robes, and ever since they have been called "Small."

It will be noticed that each tribe has a few gentes which are common to one or both of the other tribes. This is caused by persons leaving their own tribe to live with another one, but instead of uniting with some gens of the adopted tribe, they have preserved the name of their ancestral gens for themselves and their descendants. It is not probable that the names of the gentes are very ancient. The Blood gentes "Many horses" and "Many children" are neither of them thirty years old. The Piegan gens "Stifftops" is also a comparatively new name. Each gens is governed by a chief chosen by the ceremony of the "Medicine Lodge" which will be described in another place. However, it can hardly be said that chiefs *govern* the gentes. Matters of importance relating to a gens only are discussed by majority. Matters of less consequence, such as the disputes about the ownership of a horse, a family quarrel, or a theft, are carried straight to the chief for his decision. Subjects of importance to the tribe are discussed in the centrally located council, a decision is rendered by the majority. A tribal council is attended by all the chiefs, medicine men and married warriors of the tribe. A council is called "they-all-talk," a tribal and a gentile council house "in-the-middle-talk-to-each-other-house."

The Blackfeet have very few laws for the social and military government of the people. The law regarding murder is, that the murderer must be killed by some of the male relatives of the murdered; if the murderer escapes, some of his male relatives may be killed in his place. If a married man, who has no near relatives dies, the widow may demand some warrior of his gens to avenge him. Thus, in the story of "Red Old Man," which is as follows:

> "And some widows, whose husband had been killed by the Crows, painted their faces black and came to the lodge of Red Old Man, saying, 'Our husband is dead, we have no one to avenge him,' and the women cried. Now Red Old Man's heart was good. He could not bear to hear the women crying, and he took his weapons and rushed out, saying, 'Cry not. I will avenge his death.'"

A woman guilty of adultery was punished for the first offense by cutting off the end of her nose; for the second offense she was killed. For lesser crimes there is no punishment save the contempt and jeers of the camp, which are dreaded as much as the penalty of death. A coward, one who will not go on war expeditions, is made to wear the dress of a woman, and is not allowed to braid his hair. His relatives cast him off, and he leads a miserable life, begging from lodge to lodge and sleeping with the dogs.

As the members of a gens are all relatives, however remote, men are prohibited from marrying within it, they must seek wives from some other gens. Polygamy is practiced. All the younger sisters of a man's wife are his potential wives. If he does not choose to marry them, he must be consulted regarding their disposal to other men. There is no marriage ceremony. A man having found a woman he thinks will suit him, sends one of his friends to her parents' lodge, when, in a roundabout way, he is praised for his valor, good heart, etc.

After an interval of a few days the friend is again sent to make a formal demand for the woman. The parents of the woman then call a family council to discuss the advisability of letting the young man have her. Often a price is set—a number of horses, valuable finery, etc. If within his means, the young man pays it, whereupon the bride is escorted by some female friend to his lodge, where she immediately enters upon her duties as if she had always been accustomed to them.

If a man dies his widows may become the wives of his eldest brother. However, if he does not choose to marry them, they are at liberty to marry any one else. If a man wishes to divorce his wife, he accomplishes it by taking back the price he paid for her. The woman is then at liberty to marry again. The first woman a man marries is called his "sits-beside-him-wife;" she is invested with authority over all the other wives, and does little but direct the work of the other wives and attend to her husband's wants. Her place in the lodge is on the right side of her husband's seat. She enjoys the great privilege of being allowed—to a certain extent—to participate in the conversation of the men, and often, at informal gatherings, take a whiff out of the pipe as it is being smoked around the circle.

Female children are generally named by their mothers or some female relative. Male children by their fathers or some male relative or friend. Females can always be distinguished from male names by the terminations, thus: Antelope-woman, Sitting-up-in-the-air woman, etc. As soon as a young man has taken part in some brave deed he is allowed to choose a new name for himself by which he may be known for the rest of his life. However, names are considered a man's personal property, as are his bows and arrows or his shield, and are often bought and sold, large prices sometimes being paid for them. Favorite men's names are White Shield, Bear Chief, Wonderful Sun, Running Wolf, Yellow Wolf, Wolf-coming-up-the-hill, Young Bull, Water Bull, etc. A very singular custom exists among the Blackfeet, that a man must not, under any circumstances, meet or speak to his mother-in-law, and if this rule be broken, the mother-in-law may exact a heavy payment from the offender. The writer has been unable to learn any special reason for this. Some say that the sun made the law, others that it is improper for a man to meet his mother-in-law for fear she might hear him say something impolite.

Life Among the Blackfeet

Second Paper

In ancient times the Blackfeet used dogs to transport their household goods when moving camp. But the people were not then very migratory. In those days the dwellings were made of stones, sticks, mud and grass. Tradition, however, does not mention the size or shape of them. With the advent of the horse (Blackfoot *Po-n-kah-me-ta*, i.e., elk dog) all this was changed. Instead of building stationary dwellings the people made portable lodges of tanned buffalo cowskins; and, mounted on their strong ponies, roamed at will all over their vast domains. The first horses the Blackfeet possessed were stolen from the South. It is said that "those who made stone arrow points saw not horses." So it must have been at about the close of the last or the beginning of the present century that they first possessed them.

Before the days of trading posts the Blackfeet made kettles of earth, cups and ladles of mountain sheep and buffalo horns, bowls of wood, fleshers and tanning implements of flint and bone, and awls and needles of bone. Knives were made of flint, bows of mountain-sheep horn or wood, backed with sinew and sometimes with snake skin. Arrow and spear points were of flint, long, narrow and slightly barbed. The ancient dress of the men consisted of a cowskin shirt, breech-clout, belt and leggins, and a toga of cowskin or a buffalo robe.

The women wore a short-sleeved gown of cowskin, short leggins of some kind of fur, and a cowskin or buffalo robe toga.

Moccasins were made in winter of buffalo robe. In summer of cowskin with parfleche[1] soles. Necklaces, bracelets and earrings were made of animals' teeth and claws and birds' claws. White, yellow and reddish earths were used for paints.

The Indians are represented as being a silent, sullen race, seldom speaking and never laughing or joking. However true this may be of some tribes, it is certainly not true in regard to the Blackfeet. The social customs of these people are an interesting study. Let us imagine ourselves in the midst of them for a day and see how they live. It is just sunrise and the fires are being kindled; vast quantities of smoke are rising from the smoke-holes of the lodges and ascending in thin columns in the still morning air. Everywhere women may be seen carrying water and food for the morning meal. Here, close by, is a large, plain lodge. Let us enter it. As we push aside the curtain and enter with much difficulty through the small oval hole, we are greeted by the owner of the lodge with the salutation, "Enter, friend; sit," and with a wave of his hand our host motions us to a seat on his left. While he is preparing a pipe full of tobacco, let us examine the interior of the lodge. The seats, or more properly lounges, are each about seven feet long. At either end of them are inclined frame works of willows, on which as also along the entire length are spread buffalo robes. Behind, brightly painted cowskins are hung to more effectively keep out the cold air. Between the lounges, in the little triangular spaces, are piled various sacks of painted parfleche, which contain dried meat, dried berries, and different articles of general utility. Our host's seat is directly opposite the doorway; on his right are the seats of his wives; on his left, where we are sitting, are the visitors' seats. Suspended from a lodge-pole behind a long row of drying meat is a baby. It is

---

[1]Rawhide

swathed in a huge roll of furs and only its head is visible. Like most all Blackfoot babies it never cries, but restlessly rolls its great black eyes about as if seeking to understand what is going on about it. For the first year of its life the baby is kept in this roll of cloth, incapable of moving either hands or feet. At the end of that time it will be released, a straight well-formed child.

While we are smoking the pipe, we hear the owner of an adjacent lodge shouting out for a "feast," that is, giving out the invitations. He says:

Mek-ot-se-pe-tan   kit-tum-ok-o-wah
Red Eagle   you will eat

Nat-o-wap-ah   kit-tum-ok-o-wah
Blind Medicine   you will eat

Ap-pe-kun-ny   kit-tum-ok-o-wah
White Spotted Robe   you will eat

and so forth through a long list of names, and at the close adds:

Ne-oks-kum   ki-toks-o-tchis-i-po-wai

Then you will smoke and they.

He has mentioned our names in his shouted invitations, so of course, we must attend. As we enter the lodge we find we are the first arrivals, but the other guests soon come in and take their places, according to their rank, near the host or near the doorway. "Medicine" men sit next to the host. Next to them come the chiefs, warriors and old men. The young unmarried men are seldom invited to a feast. Before each guest is placed a plate of food, which is all he may have. If he does not eat it all, he may carry the remainder home with him. No food is set before the host, however; he does not eat in the presence of his guests. Every one eats slowly and a general conversation is carried on. Sometimes the talk is about the success of a war party, or again one may tell of some funny incident, at which there is a general laugh. When all have finished eating, the great stone pipe is filled with a mixture of "larb" and tobacco, and handed to the guest on the extreme right, who lights it, after which it is smoked in turn to the extreme left and then handed back to the one who lighted it, and thus kept going around the circle until it is smoked out. After three pipefulls of tobacco have been smoked, the host ostentatiously knocks out the ashes and says, "Kyi!" whereupon the guests arise and file out of the lodge. All day this feasting is kept up, and often far into the night.

While the men thus while away the hours in feasting and smoking, the women may be seen steadily at work, tanning robes or skins, drying meat or berries, or making moccasins. The children pass their time in mimic warfare and dancing, or making mud images of men and animals. If in winter, they may be seen sliding or spinning tops on the ice. The tops are made of bulls' horns, and are kept in motion by whipping with pliable thongs. These children may be seen in the middle of the winter, playing on the ice and snow without clothing or moccasins. If they become sick nature is their only physician, but nature's work is hindered by the incessant drumming and singing which is kept up until the patient either dies or recovers. Only the stongest constitutions can successfully buffet the ills of the Blackfoot childhood. Is not this a good illustration of the survival of the fittest?

Gambling is a favorite amusement. On pleasant days the men have an outdoor game which is very popular. The small wooden wheel used is about four inches in diameter. It has five spokes, and on these are strung different sizes and colors of beads. At each end of a level space logs are placed about thirty feet apart. The wheel is rolled back and forth between these logs by two players, who throw arrows at it. Whichever first succeeds in bringing his arrow in contact with a certain spoke which has been agreed upon wins the game.

The only other game the Blackfeet have is what we call "kill the button." It is played by both sexes. When only men play, a large lodge is cleared, and an equal number of players take their places on each side of the lodge. In front of them are placed rails on which time to the gambling song is beaten with sticks. Each man bets with the one directly opposite him, and the stakes are piled up in a heap on the ground.

Some skillful player now takes two little bones, one white and the other painted red. As the song is begun he deftly tosses the bones from one hand to the other, rubs his palms together and finally holds out both hands for the one opposite to guess which contains the red bone. The winner then takes the bones, and thus the game is kept going, first one side losing then the other, and sometimes it is kept up for a night and day. The bets vary in value from a necklace to two or three horses. This gambling song is the most weird tune the writer ever heard. At first it is a scarcely audible murmur, like the gentle sloughing of an evening breeze, then it increases in volume and reaches a pitch unattainable by most voices, sinks quickly to a low bass sound, rises and falls like waves and finally dies away.

But when the sun has gone down, and darkness spread her sable mantle over the land, then the Blackfoot camp may be said to have fairly waked up. Bright fires are kindled in every lodge. The sound of drum, song, and laughter fills the air. The Indian dogs, which have dozed on the sunny sides of the lodges during the day have also waked up, and mock their brethren in the darkness beyond with long drawn, melancholy howls. In one lodge may be seen a group of old men, smoking the great stone pipes, and telling of the "deeds of other days." In several lodges, professional story tellers are entertaining large audiences with tales of the past and stories of the adventures of the ancient men and animals. As the speakers become interested in the stories they are relating, they rise to their feet, and with wonderfully perfect gesticulation and voice, imitate the movements and speech of the characters in their legends. Grouped about them sit the dusky listeners, never moving nor speaking except to laugh at some funny part of the story. So spellbound are they at the rhythmic voice and movement of the speaker that the men forget to keep the pipe lit, and the women drop the half-sewed moccasin from their motionless hands.

There, in another lodge, a party of young men are going through a war dance preparatory to a raid on the horses of some neighboring tribe. In another lodge a party of men and women are having a social dance. Near the doorway sit the musicians, who beat time to the dance song on drums made of rawhide stretched over a hoop. On one side of the lodge stand the men, on the other the women. As the drumming begins all sing and dance. The "step" is a double bending of the knees. Occasionally a woman will dance over to one of the men, and deftly throwing her toga over both their heads, give him a hearty kiss, whereupon there is a general burst of laughter. For this favor the man is expected to make the woman a present of some little article of finery. Standing by the fire are huge bowls of food of which the dancers partake at intervals. Such was the life of the Blackfeet when the writer first knew them. With plenty of buffalo meat for food, and plenty of buffalo robes for clothing, no people were happier than they. But now, surrounded by a strange race which is driving the game from their land and depriving them of their means of sustenance, what wonder that they are silent and sullen?

Life Among The Blackfeet

Third Paper

The Blackfeet are pre-eminently a prairie people. The great canyons and wooden slopes of their mountains are unknown to them. On the prairie, however, from the Saskatchewan to the Yellowstone, there is not a streamlet or slough by which they have not pitched their lodges. The reason for this is that it has always been much easier to kill buffalo than mountain animals, and as buffalo have always been found near their camp, they have never been obliged to clamber over the mountains in search of food. Again, the mountains have always been inhabited by hostile tribes, which, although no match for the Blackfeet on the prairie, could totally destroy them once they penetrated the timbered defiles of their mountain home.

In a former number of the *Forest and Stream* the writer has described the manner in which the Blackfeet used to catch buffalo.[1] Another ingenious method of hunting was the *Pis-tsis-tse-kay* for catching eagles. Perhaps of all the articles used for personal adornment, eagle feathers were the most highly prized. They were not only used to decorate head dresses, garments and shields, but they were held as a standard of value. A few lodges of people in need of eagle feathers

---

[1]See pages 18-20.

would leave the main camp and move up close to the foot-hills, where eagles are generally more numerous than out on the prairie. Having arrived at a good locality, each man selected a little knoll or hill, and with a stone knife and such other rude implements as he possessed dug a pit in the top of it large enough for him to lie in. Within arm's length of the mouth of the pit he securely pegged a wolfskin to the ground, which had previously been stuffed with grass to make it look as life-like as possible. Then, cutting a slit in its side, he inserted a large piece of tough bull meat and daubed the hair about the slit with blood and liver.

In the evening, when all had returned to camp, an eagle dance was held in which every one participated. Eagle songs were sung, whistles made of eagle wing-bones were blown, and the "medicine men" prayed earnestly for success. The next morning the men arose before daylight, and smoked two pipes to the sun. Then each one told his wives and all the women of his family not to go out or look out of the lodge until he returned, and not to use an awl or needle at any kind of work, for if they did the eagles would surely scratch him, but to sing the eagle songs and pray for his good success.

Then, without eating anything, each man took a human skull and repaired to his pit. Depositing the skull in one end of it, he carefully covered the mouth over with slender willows and grass, and lying down, pillowed his head on the skull, and waited for the eagles to come. With the rising of the sun came all the little birds, the good for nothing birds, the crows, ravens and hawks, but with a long sharp pointed stick the watcher deftly poked them off the wolf skin. The ravens were most persistent in trying to perch on the skin, and every time they were poked off would loudly croak. Whenever an eagle was coming the watcher would know it, for all the little birds would fly away, and shortly an eagle would come down with a rush and light on the ground. Often it would sit on the ground for a long time pruning its feathers and looking about. During this time the watcher was earnestly praying to the skull and to the sun to give him power to capture the eagle, and all the time his heart was beating so loudly that he thought the bird would surely hear it. At last, when the eagle had perched on the wolf skin and was busily plucking at the tough bull meat, the watcher would cautiously stretch out his hands and grasping the bird firmly by the feet, quickly bear it down the cave, where he crushed in its breast with his knee.

The deadfall was another contrivance the Blackfeet had for catching animals, especially wolves. It is possible, however, that the early fur traders taught them how to make it. The running noose was extensively used at the *Pis-kans* for catching wolves. Antelope were caught in a manner like that practiced by some African tribes: long lines of bushes were stuck up on the prairie like the initial letter V, and from there they were quickly scared on into the pit, after which they were killed and the meat distributed among the hunters.

Meat was the principal diet of the Blackfeet. They either ate it fresh by boiling or roasting it, or they dried it and made it into pemmican, which consists of finely pounded dry meat, grease and berries. Every summer vast quantities of berries were dried and preserved for winter use. Blackfoot delicacies were pemmican, dried tongue and back fat, marrow guts and "boss ribs," but perhaps the greatest of all delicacies was an unborn buffalo calf.

In ancient times the Blackfeet cultivated but one plant, the tobacco. This plant is not indigenous to the Northwest, but it is easy to conceive how the Blackfeet came to possess it. The tribes were not always at war with each other; treaties were often made which remained unbroken for years, and during those years of peace a lively intertribal commerce was carried on. Thus in time the tobacco plant was carried from tribe to tribe westward to the land of the Blackfeet, and perhaps even across the Rockies to the tribes on the Pacific Slope.

The writer was told not long ago by an old Cree Indian that his people used to make yearly journeys from the north

Saskatchewan to the Yellowstone to exchange their furs with southern tribes for paint. A good illustration of Indian commerce.

Life Among The Indians

Fourth Paper

The Blackfeet divide the year into two seasons, winter, *sto-ye*, meaning "closed," and summer, *na-pos*, meaning "open." These seasons are subdivided into months, a month being the length of a moon—about twenty-eight days. Different phases of the moon are termed:

New moon—*An-nuk-nium*, or "in sight."

Half moon—*Stahk-tsi-kya-nuk-nium*, or "half in sight."

Full moon—*Ksis-tos-im*, or "round."

Last quarter—*E-ne*, or "dead."

Different seasons of the year are termed: Spring—"grass starts up;" early summer—"make lodges;" midsummer— "berries ripe;" autumn—"leaves drop;" early winter— "water freezes;" midwinter—"very cold." The people have no idea how many months constitute a year. One old fellow told the writer that winter has seven months and summer nine. It is customary to note the duration of any important event by counting the days with sticks.

The cardinal points of the compass are named: North— *Ap-put-os-ohts*, "behind direction;" South—*Am-skap-ohts*, "ahead direction;" East—*Pe-nap-ohts*, "low direction," and West—*Ah-met-ohts*, "up direction." Intermediate points such as Southwest, Northeast, etc., are not recognized. Speaking of the wind, it is said to be going *to* a certain direction, not coming from.

The class names for animals are exceedingly interesting. Three great classes are recognized: First, *Spuhts-ah-pek-seks*, or "above animals," including everything which flies; second, *So-ohts-uh-pek-seks*, or "beyond animals," including all strictly land animals; third, *Kse-ohts-uh-pek-seks*, or "under animals," including fishes, lizards, crabs, "pollywogs," turtles and the beaver and otter.

Animals are named from peculiarity of habit, motion, color or shape which they possess and some from the sound which they make. Antelope and deer are collectively named *Ah-wa-kas*, meaning "runners." Distinctively, the antelope is called "prairie runner," the white-tail deer, "swaying tail," and the black-tail, "black-tail." The beaver is called "the tree biter" and the otter "wind hair," its fur being used to wind around scalp locks. Buffalo are termed *e-ne-uh*, which is very nearly the same as *e-ne* the word for death. Ducks generally are called "red feet." The owl is named "all ears," the bull bat "fighter." The chicadee (*Parus atricapillus*) is called *ne-po-muk-i* for does it not always keep saying *ne-po-muk-i! ne-po-muk-i!* "Summer is coming! Summer is coming." There is not a single quadruped to be found in the country for which the Blackfeet have not a name. But many of the birds, especially the migratory ones, are not named other than to be called "little animals."

All birds and quadrupeds are supposed to have languages as well as men. Of all the animals, the geese are said to be most intelligent. "They have chiefs who go ahead and watch out for good camping grounds, where there is plenty of food, and where no enemies are to be found." Of all quadrupeds, the beaver is considered the most intelligent. He works in the summer and in the winter he has a warm hole, plenty of food, and does nothing but eat, dance, sing and sleep.

The Blackfeet profusely decorate parfleche sacks, robes, skins, etc. with brightly painted designs. Figures having sharp angles are the most common. Many note the history of their brave deeds in pictographs on large cow skins. Battles, war expeditions, the number of scalps taken, are represented, and the whole is interspersed with pictures of the different "medicine" animals the person has seen or killed. When the Blackfeet make a picture of a mammal, bird, or reptile, they generally draw a line from the mouth to the center of the body and then make a triangular figure to represent the heart. In the February number of the *Popular Science Monthly* is an article on a prehistoric cemetery. Figure 20 representing part of the drawing of an animal, has the line extending from the mouth backward. Unfortunately the piece of rock on which the animal is drawn, has been broken; were it complete, the triangular figure at the end of the line would undoubtedly be seen. According to some illustrations by Mr. Frank Cushing, in the February *Century*, the Zunis of New Mexico also represent the hearts of animals in their pictographs; thus it will be seen that the Blackfeet, the Zunis, and a tribe which was extinct several hundred years ago, had a common method of picturing animals.

The Blackfeet have a great many different songs. They are, however, songs without words, save one drinking song about the old man. The writer has endeavored to sing these songs and to repeat them on the violin, but has wholly failed. Nor has he ever met a white man who could repeat one of them.

The musical scale of the Blackfeet is quite different from ours, only a few of the bass sounds can be produced on the piano, the higher ones not at all. As the songs are nearly all of a sacred nature, they will be particularized in another place.

Life Among The Blackfeet

Fifth Paper

"The method of Mythological Philosophy," says that eminent ethnologist, Major J.W. Powell, "is this: All the phenomena of the outer objective world are interpreted by comparison with those of the inner subjective world. Whatever happens, someone does it; that someone has a will and works as he wills. The basis of the philosophy is personality. The persons who do the things which we observe in the phenomena of the universe are the gods of mythology—*the cosmos is a pantheon*. Under this system, whatever may be the phenomena observed, the philosopher asks 'Who does it?' and 'Why?' and the answer comes 'A god with his design.' The actors in mythologic philosophy are gods." Thus in the mythologic philosophy of the Blackfeet: In the beginning was a great womb in which everything was conceived, animals, trees, man, everything was in this womb and they fought continually to see who should be born first. Once when they fought furiously, they burst the womb, and a man jumped out first. So all the animals and everything called him Old Man, and he named them my Young Brothers. The Old Man made the people, but instead of putting hands on them, he put on claws like the bears, and they dug roots and ate berries for food. In those days the buffalo used to drive the people into *pis-kans*, and then kill and eat them. One day the

Old Man came along when the buffalo were feasting on them, and when he saw what they were doing, he sat down and cried and tore his hair. And he said: "I have badly made the people, they cannot defend themselves." And he went to where were yet a few people, and with his stone knife slit their paws, making fingers thereon. And he taught them to make bows and arrows, and knives. And he made their right arms the strongest that they might bend the bow with great force. He talked to the people, saying: "When the buffalo again come to drive you into the *pis-kan*, go quietly and hide your weapons under your robes. When you have come into the *pis-kan*, then draw your bows and shoot rapidly." And the people did as they had been told. The first arrow that was shot struck a buffalo in the side, and he cried out "Oh! my brothers, a great fly bites me. I die;" and he fell to the ground and died. And the people shot many more buffalo, and they cried out "Great flies bit through us," and they fell and died.

The buffalo yet alive found that the people were shooting them, and they said: "You people! you people! do not kill us; we will never eat any more of you." then the Old Man, who was sitting on a rock looking on, said to them "Hold on, hold on; we will gamble to see which shall be eaten." So he cried out to all the animals to come and help the people gamble against the buffalo, and they all came—all the birds and animals came. First, the elk gambled with the buffalo and lost, the different animals in turn gambled against the buffalo and each one lost. Now on the third day all the animals had lost except one which had not yet gambled. The little mouse's turn has now come, and when he took the bones in his little paws (the game was "kill the bones") all the animals and the people shouted. "Take courage little mouse, take courage little mouse." Then the little mouse took courage and made his little paws go so fast that the buffalo knew not which one of them held the bone, and they guessed the wrong one, whereupon the people shouted loudly and quickly stringing their bows, they shot a number of fat cows and gave a feast to all the animals, and the Old Man gave the mice the buffalo heads to live in. To this day they make their homes in them; so are they rewarded for saving the people.

The Old Man, the maker of the people, is a god[1] but he is not the chief god; the sun holds that position. Perhaps the best way to give the Blackfoot idea of the sun will be to translate the legend of the origin of *O-kan*, or what is known among the frontiersmen as the "medicine lodge." It is as follows.

Now in those days a man fell sick; for a long time he lay in his bed because of his sickness, and his wives and relatives said, "His sickness is of the regular kind; he will surely die;" and they cried unceasingly. In the night a spirit came to the sick man, when he slept, and it said to him, "Come, let us go to the Sun and ask him to take pity on you, and you may recover." So the soul of the sick man went with the spirit to the Sun. And when they came to the Sun's lodge they dare not enter, but sat down by the doorway on the ground, and covered their heads with their robes. At night when the Sun returned home he saw the spirit and the sick man sitting by the doorway of his lodge, and he said to them, "Rise and enter, for the night is cold;" and when they were come in he said. "Why have you come?" and the spirit said to him, "Oh, Sun, pity him! pity him! his body is sick; make him well." And the Sun for a long time did not speak. Then he said, "Go back and make a lodge like mine. Have your head wife make the lodge, and all the people help you. You shall call it *O-kan*" (his sleep), and then he told the soul of the sick man everything to do, and the soul went back to its body.

In the morning the sick man arose and ate, and his relations were very glad to see him well again, and they told him "your recovery is very strange." "True, true," he said, and he told them about his going to the Sun, and they began to make a lodge as the Sun had directed them. The man who had been sick and his head wife went up on a hill and smoked and prayed to the Sun, and the young men, all the hunters, killed many buffalo and brought the tongues to them. And all the women of the

---

[1]The Old Man, according to anthropologists, was not a god, although he may have had supernatural powers. The authenticity of the legend on pages 63 and 64 has also been questioned.

camp who had not committed adultery came and helped to cut and dry the tongues, and if any woman helped who had committed adultery, and any man knew it, he cried out quickly, and they immediately killed her, for so the Sun had said. No woman who had committed adultery was allowed to help make the *O-kan*. Now when many hundred tongues had been dried and plenty of berries gathered, the women began to build the lodge. First they built a high circular wall of upright poles and then made a peaked roof of smaller sticks and covered it with brush. When the lodge was built and much firewood had been gathered, the sick man who recovered and his wives brought all the dried tongues and berries, and much other food into it, and they slept there that night.

The morrow was the first day of the week. All the men wore their war shirts and war head-dresses, and brought with them their weapons, their bows and arrows, spears, knives, shields, and their trophies of war; all their brave deeds they brought with them. First entered the lodge the head chief, and after him came the "medicine men," the under chiefs and warriors, according to their rank. Now when all were come into the lodge who could be seated, the "medicine men" took choice portions of the tongues and other food which had been prepared, and put it all in a hole in the ground for the Sun, and they sung the "medicine song," for so had the Sun said to do.

There was a "medicine" pipe filled and held aloft to the Sun, and a medicine man prayed saying "O Sun, take pity O Old Man! take pity, let us survive, let us survive. Let our lives (be) full; let us survive, let us (be) old. Old men, young men, women and little children, pity them all; let their lives (be) full. Give us our eating, let us not starve. We have built a lodge for you, a big lodge; let us survive. Keep the ghosts away; keep our enemies from coming upon us; let us see them far off. Give us good hearts; give us good lives, all you Above-People. O Sun, we have built a lodge for you and we give you (to) eat. Look at us, pity us; pity us." (All the people) "Ah-h-h-h-h-h! pity take, pity take."

Every one who came to the *O-kan* brought presents and hung them on the walls. Each person, even the little children, gave (to) the Sun. Quivers of bows and arrows were given, shields, war head-dresses, war shirts, spears, scalps, bags of colored earth, fine fins, eagle feathers, everything was given. If any one had killed a white buffalo, he brought the robe and gave it (to) the Sun, saying: "Here is your very own; I ate not the meat, not even the tongue. I gave you the meat long ago, there now is the robe, take it and pity me, give me full life, let me (be) old."

Now, when all the presents had been given to the Sun, each warrior in turn counted his "coup"—that is, his successes in war. For instance, one would say: "The Sweet Grass Hills, that place we fought the Crees. I killed three; two bows I took. My friends there, Bear's-Paw and Heavy-Runner, saw me. I took the scalps." Singularly enough, the taking of a scalp does not count a "coup," neither does the killing of an enemy. To count a "coup" the person must take a bow or weapon or the horse of an enemy, and must have witnesses present to prove it. He must also bring with him the arms by which he counts his "coups." Every time a "coup" is counted the musicians—the drummers—beat their drums, and all the people loudly shout the name of the one who counts it. The number of "coups" a person counts are accurately counted and remembered. The head chief of the tribe is the one who has counted the most "coups."[1] Whenever he dies, or when he becomes too old to go to war, the one who has counted the most "coups" next to him becomes the head chief. The chief of a gens is the warrior who, of all others belonging to the gens, has counted the most "coups."

Now, when all the "coups" had been counted, all the young men who had been in battle for the first time were made warriors. Slits were cut in their backs, and cords passed through them, to which were attached buffalo heads, and the young men ran a long ways, dragging the heads by the slits in their backs, and if any one cried out

---

[1]This is erroneous. Some head chiefs, such as Crowfoot, were known to have had modest war records. And to say that the head chief was automatically chosen because of the number of war exploits is also erroneous.

or would not run, he could not become a warrior.[1] Women, too, came into the lodge, and they wore clothes like the one of whom they would speak. Their hair was dressed the same and they were painted like him, and they touched the Sun's things and were told what brave deed the one of whom they spoke must do that they might always love and honor him.

Now, when all these ceremonies had been done, generally at the close of the third day, the people returned to their lodges and the medicine men only remaind behind, to whom came the sick that they might survive. The medicine men cured them. After that the *O-kan* was left and no one could come near it, or take away the presents which hung on it, for everything belonged to the Sun. And after this, when a man was very sick, and even the "medicine men" were not sure they could save him, then would the head wife of the sick man put on a garment of cowskin only, and barefooted, she would walk all about among the lodges saying loudly: "Take pity Sun! very sick lies my husband. You have seen my ways; you know that I am not guilty of any sin. Pity take and make my husband well; I will build you a lodge; I will make the *O-kan*. We all will build the *O-kan* and make you presents. Hear me, hear me, and give us full lives." So it happens that every summer when the berries are ripe that a lodge is built for the Sun. Sometimes only one woman promises to build it, and again, many women make the promise.

The building of the *O-kan* and the attending ceremonies is designed for three purposes: first, any woman who has been unfaithful to her husband is then pretty sure to be exposed and killed, and in this way adultery is suppressed to a great extent; second, the lodge is built for the Sun, the wonderful Above-People, and the Old Man—it is an offering to the gods; third, the public counting of the "coups" is designed to stimulate the warriors to brave deeds, that they may receive the plaudits of the people. A chieftainship is an enviable position among the Blackfeet, and can only be obtained by most indomitable courage in war.

---

[1]This is also inaccurate. In fact, a young man vowed to go through the self-torture ritual if a male member of his family was in danger of losing his life. It was really a ceremony of thanks.

Life Among The Blackfeet

Sixth Paper

The religion of the Blackfeet is a strange mixture of three stages of mythologic philosophy. It consists of remnants of *Hecastotheism*, and complete *Zootheism*, and, to a certain extent, *Physitheism*.

So far as the writer knows, only three inanimate things are worshipped now by the Blackfeet, but there is conclusive evidence that their religion was once pre-eminently hecastotheistic, that is, that they worshipped trees, rivers, mountains, rocks, in fact, all inanimate things. There is a certain fossil found in the bluffs along the rivers which is much the shape of a buffalo. It is called *e-nis-kim*, buffalo rock, and is worshipped by all. It is sometimes hung on the necks of little children as a necklace, but is more frequently deposited in the "medicine" sacks of the "medicine men." The legend of it is as follows:

> Long ago, in the winter time, the people were starving, for no buffalo could be found. The young men went out to hunt every day, but not even a poor old bull could they find. They waited and waited for the buffalo to come, saying: "Surely they will be here to-morrow," but they did not come; and at last the people were so hungry and weak they could not move the camp. Now, one day a young married man killed a jack rabbit, and he hastened it home and said to one of his wives: "Go, quickly now and get some water, we will cook this rabbit and eat it." When the young women was going down the path to

the river she heard something singing, and she looked about to see what it was. There, jammed into a crevice of the bark on a cotton-wood tree, was a stone (the e-nis-kim), and with it a few buffalo hairs, for there had a buffalo rubbed himself. And the woman was afraid and dared not go past the tree. And the *e-nis-kim* sang a beautiful song, and the woman stood and listened. And when it had finished, it said "Take me to your lodge, and when it is dark call all the people and teach them to sing my song. Pray, too, that you may not starve; that the buffalo may come, and when it is once more day your hearts will be glad." So the woman took the *e-nis-kim* home and gave it to her husband, telling him all that occurred. In the evening all the people came and learned the song and prayed, and while it was yet dark they heard the buffalo coming. Many came, and the sound of their running was like thunder, and as soon as it was daylight the hunters went out and killed many fat cows, and the peoples' hearts were glad.

Another object of hecastotheistic worship is a large red and white colored rock lying on the side of a hill some five miles above Fort Conrad on the Marias River. It was once on the very top of the hill, but successive raining seasons have gradually washed the loose soil from under it, so that each year it moves down a few feet. The Blackfeet regard this as a supernatural power and consequently worship it. Seldom does one pass by it without making it a present of a bracelet, or string of beads, or something of more or less value.

The middle butte of the Sweet Grass hills is also worshipped. The worship, however, partakes more of fear than veneration. It is said that if any one happens to camp by it, that it will appear to him in his dreams and ask him for a woman, promising in payment some of the game which is so plentiful on its slopes. Camps are never pitched at its base, and any one hunting about it must make it a present.

It is not unlikely that there are more objects of Blackfoot hecastotheistic worship than the ones given above, but as yet the writer is unacquainted with them.

Zootheism forms an important part of the Blackfoot religion. Still, the animal gods hold but a secondary place among the wonderful beings, the rulers of the universe. Each Indian has his own secret god, either an animal or a star, or constellation of stars. Having arrived at the age when he may go on the warpath, each young man goes out on the prairie or to some lonely spot by himself, and then fasts for four days and four nights. Whatever he dreams of, as he lies in a half insensible state, he takes for his god, for his secret helper. But the Blackfoot's prayers are not directly to this secret helper. The wonderful animal which he takes for his own god is not directly asked to fulfill his wishes. Animals are supposed to be much nearer the supreme gods (the Sun, Moon, Old Man, and the Stars) than mortal man, and the secret helper is implored to ask the supreme gods to grant whatever the Indian may pray for.

Of the physitheistic gods, the Sun stands at the head; next to him in power is his wife, the Moon, and after them the Morning Star, their son, named *E-pi-su-ahts*—early riser. In the mythic tales which will close this paper, the reader will find accounts of the doings of the wonderful animal gods and bright people of the sky.

The soul, that part of the person which never dies, is supposed by a Blackfoot to be his shadow. After death this shadow leaves the body and travels to the Sand Hills, a large barren tract of prairie some thirty miles beyond the Sweet Grass hills. Here, living in lodges which are not visible to the mortal eye, are all the Blackfeet who ever lived on earth. Their daily occupations are the same as those they pursued on earth. "Still," said an old fellow to me once, "what a life-for-nothing life it must be. Their bones have no meat on them, their horses and dogs are only skeleton dogs and horses, and they hunt, kill and eat skeleton buffalo. But," continued the old fellow, "how useless it must be to eat only what looks like the shadow of meat."

Before death the shadow is called *kwo-tuck*; after death it takes the form of the skeleton and is then named *sta-au*. Although the Sand Hills are the homes of the many dead, the *sta-auks*, or, as we may translate it, the ghosts, do not always live there. They have the power to come and go unseen, and often visit the spots which were dear to them, and it is thought that they are always present at a death to lead the new ghost to his future home. A ghost also is capable of avenging any wrong which may have been done to him before death. Sometimes he will come and whistle over the lodge of any one he hates; sometimes he shoots invisible arrows, which quickly kill any one whom they may hit. Enemies, who have been killed and scalped, are thought to be specially invested with this power of shooting invisible arrows. Not long ago the Cree Indians made a raid on the horses belonging to this place, and in the fight which ensued two of them were killed and scalped by the Blackfeet. A few days since, a little child—belonging to one of the Blackfeet who were in the fight—was taken suddenly sick and died in a few hours. The reason assigned for its death was that the ghost of one of the fallen Crees had shot it.

Every person, after death, is supposed to go to the Sand Hills. The good and the bad are both certain to go. The "happy hunting grounds" of another world are unknown to the Blackfeet. Their idea of a future life is a dreary, everlasting make-believe existence, a pantomime of the life in this world.

Disease is supposed to be caused by the many evil ghosts which are constantly hovering about, seeking an opportunity to take life. These ghosts have many ways of causing death. Sometimes they shoot their invisible arrows; sometimes they cause small, unseen animals to enter persons and eat their vital parts, again they kill by degrees, causing one to suffer and linger for a long time in great agony; and sometimes they commence at the feet and kill one slowly, every day killing up toward the body a little further until death at last ensues.

When a person dreams, the Blackfeet believe that his shadow has in reality been away from his body and actually participated in the acts of which he has dreamed. The dream is thought to be a special gift from the gods, thus enabling man to look forward into the future and ward off any danger that may be threatening him. If a man dreams that he has seen a person long since dead, he immediately on waking makes a present to the gods to pay them for the good fortune which they may give him. Thus, no matter of what one dreams about, it is sure to be interpreted either for good or bad.

Life Among The Blackfeet

Seventh Paper

The Blackfeet medicine practices consist chiefly of incantations. Some few roots and herbs are used, and bleeding and blistering is also practiced.

In Blackfoot a "medicine man" is called a Bear man and a "medicine pipe" a bear-pipe. The bear, the wonderful monster, most powerful of all the animals, is thought to be—like strange white buffalo—the special property of the gods. Whenever a person killed one he left the meat as an offering, and took only the claws for the necklace, and a small piece of the hide to wrap around the bear pipe. Any one but a Bear man terms the bear *Ki-yu*. The Bear man, however, must never use this word, the name for the animal being *Nampska*. Unfortunately, the writer has been unable to learn the meaning of either of these words. A bear-pipe is in reality no pipe at all, merely a very long wooden pipe stem, beautifully wrapped and decorated with pieces of all kinds of fur, scalps, and many colored feathers. When in use any large pipe-bowl is smoked which will fit the stem. When not in use it is rolled up in fur, and in pleasant weather hung on a tripod outside. At other times it is kept suspended on a lodge pole just above the seat of the owner. A large quantity of tobacco and herb is always kept with the bear-pipe, and besides this, the following articles which are used in the pipe ceremonies: A strip of white buffalo robe, which is placed around the forehead of the Bear-man, one or more rattles, the dried scrotum of a buffalo bull filled with small pebbles, a pair of wooden tongs, a bag of red paint, another of sweet grass, and a string of bells made of dried buffalo hoofs.

When not in use, no one may touch a bear-pipe except the Bear-man, *Nanp-skan*, and his head wife, the Bear-woman, between it and the fire; fire or ashes may not be carried out of the lodge, and the wood in the fireplace must be laid so that the sticks touch each other in the center, the long ends projecting away from the pipe. When a person enters a Bear-pipe-man's lodge he must, on leaving, go out by the same side of the lodge by which he entered. For instance, if one should pass by the right side of the lodge, thus making a complete circle around the pipe, he would be sure to have some bad luck befall him. Months frequently pass during which the pipe is not unrolled. Certain occasions only warrant this important ceremony. At the *o-kan*, as before stated, the bear-pipes are smoked, and again, the first time thunder is heard in the spring. A bear-pipe is valued equal to from ten to fifteen or more head of horses, and frequently is bought and sold. If a man possessing one of these pipes dies, the pipe and all its appurtenances is buried with him. The writer has never witnessed the ceremonies at the changing of ownership of a pipe, and is unable to say whether the pipe is then smoked or not.

Only within the last few weeks has the writer been able to learn anything at all of the ceremonies and duties of the Bear-men, and only after repeated disavowal of all belief in the white man's God was he allowed to witness the peculiar ceremonies. The first time he was present the pipe was only unwrapped, the occasion being the healing of a sick woman. The Bear-pipe man was an old gray-headed man. When I entered the lodge it was already well filled with men who had been invited to participate in the ceremony.[1] Between

[1] All of the material commencing with the words "When I entered" and extending through page 60 were borrowed verbatim by Grinnell. See pages 279-281 of Blackfoot Lodge Tales.

the aged Bear-man, and his wife, the Bear-woman, was the pipe, as yet unrolled, lying on a carefully folded buffalo robe. Plates of food were placed before each guest, and when all had eaten and a common pipe had been lighted, the ceremony commenced. With the wooden tongs (made of a forked branch of willow) the woman took a large coal of fire from the fireplace and dropped it on the ground directly before the bear-pipe. Then, while every one joined in singing a pipe song, a beautiful low, plaintive chant, she took a bunch of dried, sweet grass and, alternatively raising and lowering her hand in time to the music, at last dropped it on the coal. As the thin column of perfumed smoke rose from the burning herb, both she and the Bear-man leaned over it and, grasping handfuls of it, rubbed it over their persons to purify themselves before touching the sacred pipe. They also took each a small piece of some kind of root from a little bag and ate it, signifying that they purified their bodies, not only on the outside, but on the inside.

The man and woman now faced each other and began the Buffalo song, keeping time to the music by touching with their clenched hands—the right and left alternatively—the wrappings of the pipe. Occasionally, they would make the sign for buffalo—viz., both hands—tightly closed—elevated to and touching the sides of the head, forefinger of each crooked obliquely forward to represent the horns. After singing this song for some ten minutes they changed the tune to the Antelope song; and instead of touching the pipe wrappings with the clutched hands, which represented the walking of buffalo, they closed the hands, leaving the index finger in the form of a hook and the thumbs partly extended and in time to the music, as in the previous song, alternatively touched wrappers with the right and left hands, and occasionally brought the hands to the side of the head, making the sign for antelope, and uttered a loud Kuh! to represent the whistling or snorting of the animal.

At the conclusion of this song, the woman put another bunch of sweet grass on a coal and carefully undid the wrappings of the pipe, holding each one over the smoke that it might be pure. At last the last wrapping was removed, the Bear-man gently grasped the stem, and every one beginning to sing the Pipe song, he raised and lowered it several times, shaking it as he did so, until every feather and bit of scalp and fur could be plainly seen.

At this moment the sick woman entered the lodge and with great effort, for she was very weak, walked over to the Bear-woman and knelt down before her. The Bear-woman then produced a small bag of red paint and painted a broad band across the sick woman's forehead, a stripe down the nose, and a number of round dots on each cheek; then picking up the pipe-stem she held it up toward the sky and prayed, saying, "Listen, Old Man, take pity! Listen Sun, take pity! Listen all Above-people, Animals, Under-water-people, all take pity! Let us survive. Let us survive. Why is our daughter now sick? Give her complete life. Give us good, give us all complete lives." At the conclusion of this short prayer all the people uttered a m-m-m-m-ah! and reaching out their arms folded them across their breasts, signifying that they took the words to their hearts. Every one now commenced the Pipe-song and the Bear-woman passed the pipe-stem over different parts of the sick woman's body, after which she arose and left the lodge.

The old man then took a common pipe which had been lighted and blew three whiffs of smoke toward the sky, three to the ground and three on the bear-pipe stem, and then repeated much the same prayer as that in the ceremony of the *o-kan*. Three drums were then produced, the war song commenced, and the old man, rattle in hand, danced three times from his seat to the doorway and back. This was an entirely new dance to the writer, and was intended to imitate the movements of the bear. The old man stooped down very slightly, kept all his limbs very rigid, extended his arms like one giving a benediction, and danced back and forth in time to the music in quick, sudden steps. He then took the pipe-stem, and holding it in front of him, went through the same performance. Afterward the pipe-stem was handed to the guests, and each one holding it aloft for a few seconds made a short prayer. The person who sat on the left of the writer prayed for continuance of life for his wives and children, the person on the right prayed for success in horse stealing. This concluded the ceremony.

Schultz and son, Lone Wolf, 1884.

—Courtesy of Archives, Montana State University Libraries

Life Among The Blackfeet

Eighth Paper

Not long ago, about the 1st of May, the first thunder of the season was heard. I went immediately to a Bear-man's lodge and found him drumming and singing the Thunder song. "To-morrow, my son, to-morrow," said the old fellow as I looked in at the doorway, "we will dance, come to-morrow, I am only singing now because my heart is glad." The next day, at the proper time, with a number of other guests, I entered the lodge.

The pipe-stem had already been unrolled. In front of the fire were two huge kettles of cooked berries and a large wooden bowlful of them was given to each guest. Each one, before eating, took a few of them in his fingers and rubbed them into the ground, saying, "Take pity all Above-people, look at us."

When all had finished eating a large black stone pipe bowl was filled and fitted on the Bear-pipe-stem, the Bear-man then held it aloft and quickly repeated this prayer: "Listen, Thunder, listen, Old Man, Sun, all Above-people, all Above-animals, listen, take pity. You will smoke; the Bear-man fills his pipe. Let us not starve; make the berries large and sweet; let the bushes have a heavy load. Look at all the women and little children; look at us all; let us reach old age, let our lives be complete. Let us destroy our enemies, help the young men in the battles; man, woman, child, we all pray to you; take pity and give us good."

He then took the pipe and danced with it as in the previous ceremony. At this time another storm had come up and the thunder crashed directly over our heads. "Listen," said the Bear-man, as he stopped dancing. "It hears us; we are doing this uselessly;" and he raised his face, animated with enthusiasm, toward the sky, his whole body trembling with excitement, and holding the pipe aloft once more repeated his prayer. All the rest of the people were excited and repeatedly clasped their arms over their breasts saying, "Take pity! Good give us, good give us!" After this the pipe was handed to a guest on the right end of the circle. Another guest took a lighted brand from the fire and counted four "coups," at the end of each "coup" touching the bowl with the fire, and when he had repeated the last one the pipe was lighted. It was then smoked back and forth around the circle, each one as he received it for the first time repeating a prayer before he put the stem to his lips. When it smoked out a hole was dug in the ground, the ashes carefully knocked into it and covered over, and the Thunder ceremony ended.

When people are so sick that they cannot leave their lodge they often send for a Bear-man to come and "doctor" them. Although certain roots and herbs are used for medicine, as before stated, the most efficacious remedy is thought to be the *I-so-kin-uh-kin*, the songs for the sick. These songs are not the property of the individual or gens, but may be sung by any one. They are supposed to drive away the evil ghosts. The drum is always an accompaniment of the *I-so-kin-uh-kin*, with sometimes rattles, hoof bells and whistles. All the women of the lodge join in the singing. Sometimes the chief doctor or singer blows upon the patient through a bird's wing-bone, after each breath uttering a loud "whoo!" Water is blown in the form of spray. In cases of rheumatism, the other diseases when the pain is very often acute in certain parts of the body it is usual to bleed the place by cutting an incision or two with a knife. Blistering is done with hot rocks, and sometimes dried prickly pear thorns are inserted in the flesh, and burned, the thorn being consumed to the very point. People of one gens very seldom doctor people of another one. Although any one may be a doctor, only one or two persons in a gens—those who have been very successful with patients—have much practice. Sometimes the doctor is a man and sometimes a woman. When one of these doctors is called upon to practice on a sick person, it is customary to demand a present at the very beginning, a horse or a number of robes, after a day or two another present is exacted, and it often happens when a man's sickness is protracted that he is obliged to pay out his very last horse and other valuable property in doctor fees.

Life Among The Blackfeet

Ninth Paper

In each tribe of the nation are two painted lodges, one colored red, the other white. The owners of them, like the Bear-men, are supposed to be favorites of the gods, and able to cure sickness. The value of one of these lodges is about equal to fifteen heads of horses, and they are frequently bought and sold. The tradition regarding them is this:

Long ago, the three tribes of the Nation were camped on Bow River. One day two young men were sitting by the river making arrow shafts. Directly beneath them, where the water ran swiftly against a cut bank, was a large whirlpool. One of the young men happening to look down, saw a large lodge in the bottom of the whirlpool, and he said to his companion, "Oh look! See that beautiful lodge down there;" and his friend looked but could see nothing but the water ever whirling round and round. Then said the other, "I am going down into that lodge," and his companion tried to dissuade him, saying, "Do not go, for the River people will grasp you and you will never return." But the young man was not afraid, and pulling off his clothes, he dived into the water.

When he had got to the bottom of the river, he came to the lodge, and it was painted red, and he went round to the doorway and entered it. Only one person sat in the lodge, an old man whose hair was very white and long.

He did not speak or look up but kept singing a strange song. Hanging up, on the inside of the lodge, were many buffalo robes, fine furs, and weapons, all of them painted red, and at the doorway hung a bunch of hoof bells also painted red. Now, after a long time, the old man raised his head and he said, "On the bank of the river I was making arrows, and way down in the water I saw your lodge; and I wished to see the way you live. That is why I came." Then said the old man, "Your heart is brave, return to your people and make a lodge like mine; it shall be *Nat-os-e* (of the sun) and the Sun will be glad."

When the young man returned to the bank he found his companion weeping and calling him by name, for he thought he was drowned, and he told all that he had seen in the underwater lodge. As they stood looking down into the whirlpool the other young man saw a lodge at the bottom and quickly dived into the water. After a time he returned and told his companion of his adventure; the lodge which he found was painted white, and inside were white buffalo robes, and white furs, and white painted weapons, and there was an old man who had spoken just as the other old man had spoken to the first young man who went down. Then the young men hurried home and told what they and seen, and they each made a lodge like the ones they had found in the whirlpool.

Nearly all the different tribes of Western Indians with which the writer is acquainted, build "sweat lodges." The Blackfeet are not an exception, but it is very probable that their traditions regarding the origins of the "sweat lodge" and the purpose for which it is used are different from those of any other Indians. According to tradition, the Old Man first built a sweat lodge and told the people to do so that the sun would quickly hear their prayers.

A sweat-lodge consists of a framework of light willows, covered with cow skin. It is in the shape of a hemisphere, about three feet high and six or seven feet in diameter. In the center a small hole is dug in the ground, in which are placed red-hot rocks. Every thing being ready, those who are to take the sweat crawl inside, the cow skins are pulled tightly down, so as to exclude all circulation of air, and water is thrown on the hot rocks, causing a dense steam which makes the perspiration fairly drip from one's body. When the sweat is over (it generally lasts for an hour and a half), the cow skins are removed and the framework left for the sun, it never being used a second time. During the process of sweating, prayers are offered by the Bear-man or painted lodge man. If neither of these be present, the oldest warrior makes the prayer. Occasions for building a sweat-lodge are: To pray for the success of a war party; to pray for the recovery of persons from illness, and for a continuance of life. *E-nuks-ap-i! e-nuks-ap-i!* "Let me (be) old, let me (be) old," is the constant prayer of every Indian. Women never enter a sweat-lodge.

Mr. Joseph Kipp once told the writer that when the smallpox was raging among the Indians they would crowd into sweat lodges, take an unusually hard sweat, and then jump into the icy waters of the river. Many, he said, never reached the bank again; hundreds of them being chilled and powerless to combat the strong current were swept away.

When a war party is made up, the one most noted for his bravery and success is chosen for leader. Before starting it is the duty of the leader to build a sweat-lodge for a Bear-pipe-man and any other whom the Bear-pipe-man may invite. Prayers are offered for the success of the party, and beside the sweat-lodge the leader erects a pole on which is hung a valuable present for the sun. Each member of the war party also makes the sun a present and sometimes a sacrifice. This sacrifice consists in cutting off a long lock of hair or a piece of flesh, and sometimes a joint of a finger and giving it to the sun. Women may also make these sacrifices, the reason for so doing being that if they give the sun a piece of their body he will be glad and preserve them and their relatives from death. Every day during the absence of a war party the Bear-pipe-man mounts his horse, and rattle in hand, rides all through the camp, calling out in a loud voice the names of the absent ones. He also visits the lodges of the relatives of the absent war party and sings and prays that they may be successful, the women all joining in the songs. In the event of a war party returning with scalps of the enemy, a war dance or scalp dance is held. All the women wear the shields, weapons and finery of their husbands, and have their hair parted and their faces painted just like a man's. One or more women carry the scalps on slender poles, and have the lower half of their faces painted black. The men, most of them having drums, form into a line, and opposite them stand the women. All sing, and in time to the music the women gradually advance and come up to the men, then fall back, and again advance, and soon. When an enemy is killed near camp it is customary to bring in his feet and hands, which are shot at and kicked around by the women.

When a person dies, and as soon as life is pronounced extinct, the female relatives of the deceased securely wrap the body in cow skins and robes, and having built a stout scaffold between the branches of an adjacent tree, they fasten the corpse to it with innumerable thongs. Contrary to a statement by John Young, of the Piegan Agency, all persons—men, women and children—are buried in this manner. Sometimes, however, chiefs are buried in their own lodges. There are two ways of burying in lodges; one is to suspend the deceased on a platform high enough from the ground to prevent the wolves from reaching it; the other method, as described by Mr. Kipp, is to dig a grave directly under the accustomed sitting place of the chief. After the body has been laid in it a strong platform is built just above it and covered over with stones and dirt. The weapons of a dead person were always buried with him, and in the graves of women and children articles of housewifery and toys were always placed. At the burial place of a chief or a noted warrior several horses were generally killed. At the burial lodge of a chief which the writer once found, were the skeletons of four horses. Mourning observances devolve chiefly upon the women. The wife or mother of a deceased person lacerates the calves of her legs, cuts off her hair and a joint of a finger to show her grief. The father or husband cuts off part of his hair and goes without leggins for a number of days.

For the first few days succeeding a person's death all the near relatives of the deceased spend the greater part of the time on hills adjacent to the camp, where they sit and mourn, calling the name of the dead person over and over again, until they become so hoarse they cannot speak. After a short period the men give up mourning altogether. A wife or mother, however, mourns for a year or two, not daily, but at irregular periods.

Schultz with Indian friend.
—Courtesy of Archives, Montana State University Libraries

My First Visit To The
St. Mary Lakes[1]

Since arriving in the country, I had heard much about two large, beautiful lakes, called by the whites Chief Mountain Lakes; by the Blackfoot tribes *Puktomuksi Kimiks*, "Lakes Inside." We did not then know that in 1846 Father Lacombe, S.J., assisted by his faithful guide Hugh Monroe, had set up a cross at the foot of the lower one of the lakes and with prayer had christened them St. Mary Lakes.[2]

I remembered hearing John Healy remark that upon the high mountains around them there were plenty of ibexes. That intrigued me. I was anxious to visit the lakes particularly if the animals described by Healy really could be ibexes, ruminants that, as I had always understood, were found only in the Swiss Alps.

In October of this year 1883 came my opportunity to do that. One day there came down to the fort our friends Sol Abbot and Henry Powell, and announced that, with Charlie

---

[1]Actually published in the *Great Falls Tribune*, November 18, 1936, but inserted at this point for the sake of maintaining chronological continuity.

[2]Even by 1936 Schultz had not learned that Father Lacombe did not come to Montana until long after 1846 and that he had not, in fact, become a priest at that time.

Phemmister, Jim Rutherford, and Oliver Sandoval, employees of Indian Agent Major Young, and Charles Carter, a trapper, they were going on a hunting trip to Chief Mountain Lakes, and would I join them? Ha! I put my rifle, shotgun, and bedding into their wagon, and with plenty of provisions we set out up river. We picked up Charles Carter at Abbot's ranch, and on the following day we neared the agency, stopped at the lodge of an Indian friend, and sent him on to notify Phemmister, Rutherford, and Sandoval that we had arrived. (The Indian agent, Major Young, allowed no whites other than his employees upon the reservation; he gave out that he would arrest any white trespassers, have them tried and fined in the United States court in Helena. His reason for that we were later to learn.)

Our Indian friend and his family with whom we briefly stopped had only a little flour and some dried service berries in their lodge. He said that game had become so scarce that the hunters were often days in killing a deer or antelope, and worse, many of them had used all their cartridges and had no furs or hides with which to get more from the agency trader. We gave him ten dollars, and happily smiling, truly grateful, he and his wives hurried up to the trader's store to buy beans, bacon, baking powder, sugar and tea, provisions that, they said, they and been without since the extermination of the buffalo. In the evening, a number of prominent men of the tribe came in to visit and smoke with us and to tell of their need for food. Their condition worried me. Still, I did not then realize, as I did later, how serious the outlook was for the tribe, else, doubtless, I could have helped save many who were to die from starvation in the next few months.

Early on the following morning, avoiding the agency, we struck the big Indian trail paralleling the mountains, were joined by our three friends with team and wagon, and turned northward into country new to me. It was my first close view of the Rocky Mountains. I could not keep my eyes off them, rising so abruptly, towering so high above the plain. Had they names, I asked. "No, only that farther one in sight ahead, standing out as though in the lead of the others, its east face an almost sheer cliff." That was *Nina Istukwi*, "Chief Mountain" of the Blackfoot tribes, Abbot told me. I thought that never had a mountain been more appropriately named.

At noon we turned down into the beautiful, well-timbered valley of the Cut Bank Creek and rested for a time beside the stream. I noted that its deep, clear pools fairly teemed with trout, many of large size. Our friend Oliver Sandoval, or *Inoyimum*, ("Looks Furry"), was the son of a noted Spanish employee of the old American Fur Company and a staid, competent Pikuni woman. Of us all, he alone had ever been to Chief Mountain lakes and knew of a possible way for us to get to the lower one of them with wagons. Leaving Cut Bank Creek and following his lead, we crossed the south and then the middle fork of the Milk River, the *Kimuk Sisakta* ("Little River"), and then turned into a branch trail running north-west, and up the high, steep ridge dividing the waters of the Missouri and Hudson Bay. Having crossed the Divide, we soon made camp at a large lake on the rim of a valley of Chief Mountain lakes, the *Ahkainus Kwona Ituktai* ("Many Chiefs Gathered River") of the Blackfeet.

The evening was cloudy — a hard, west wind blowing; countless flocks of ducks were hurtling over us. I got my shotgun and some cartridges from the wagon, ran out upon a long, narrow jutting out into the lake, and began shooting into the flocks. They came and went on the west side of it, and the wind drifted those that I killed to the shore. I was soon back in camp with ten, all of them canvasback and redheads, most prized, most delicious of all the varieties of ducks. We quickly dressed them and Carter laid six of them in our Dutch oven, already heated in the fire, and, against my protest, doused them with several cups of water — I maintaining that ducks should always be roasted, he insisted that they were best when stewed. It was dark when we gathered to eat them. They were tender enough but, to me, rather flavorless. Carter said that the soup was grand. I alone refused a cup of it. The meal ended and, the dishes washed, we took to our beds. Soon after midnight my companions began complaining of severe stomach pains and went frequently to the brush. Came morning and all were weak and gaunt. An examination of the Dutch oven evidenced that the delicious duck soup that they had eaten, cup after cup, had been almost pure grease. Right then and there I gave the lake the name that it bears today: Duck Lake.

We had an early morning start from the lake, and still following the Indian trail, were soon looking at a scene so tremendous, so beautiful, that I felt that I could gaze at it forever. Straight down from us was the lower one of the two lakes; close above it, the other and longer one, from whose shores the mountains rose in grandeur to great heights. It was no wonder that the Blackfeet had named them "Lakes Inside." With all respect for the memory of Father Lacombe, I think the name he gave them is most inappropriate. It is the hope of many of us — some thousands of Indians and whites — that Mr. E.T. Scoyen, superintendent of Glacier National Park, will soon restore to them their Blackfoot name.[1]

Ours were the first wagons ever upon this branch of the great north-and-south fork of the mountain trail. As we followed it down, we were obliged here and there to cut out quaking aspens and young pine growing in it and heavily to brush several narrow, boggy streamlets in order to cross with the wagons. So going, we came at noon to the foot of the lower lake, turned up along it upon a well-used trail, and made camp on the first of the outjutting points above the outlet. We did no hunting that afternoon but in a few minutes caught, in the first pool of the river, enough trout for our supper and breakfast. To my surprise, there were three varieties of them: Mackinaws, natives, and another that I could not then identify — the Dolly Varden, as I was later to learn.

We regretted that we had not brought saddle horses with which to explore our surroundings and hunt. In lieu of them, on the following morning, we crossed the river with team and wagon at a ford a few hundred yards below the foot of the

[1]The hope has not yet been realized; they are still labeled Saint Mary lakes on modern maps.

lake. Then we picketed the horses and set out for a long, flat-topped mountain close to the west of the lake, its north end almost a sheer cliff of great height. We took to a steep, well-timbered ridge running up to the mountain and, unused to walking and climbing, soon tired; so much that arriving at the timber line, we had no desire to make the still mountain. Our friend Sandoval said that he had heard the Kootenai Indians tell of a lick close under the north cliff of the mountain that was much used by the various game animals; so, after a good rest, we set out to find it, traveling slowly, cautiously, just within the edge of the timber and scanning constantly the long, steep slope for sight of game. So doing until the east end of the cliff was straight above us, we discovered farther on a band of bighorn ewes and young leaving the timber, traveling away from us upon the bare slope, beyond range of our rifles. They were not new to me. I had seen hundreds of them on the cliffs of the Missouri River badlands, and had even killed a few. What I was looking for, was most eager to see, were John Healy's "ibexes."

Where the bighorns had left the timber we discovered the lick. It was in a shallow wide coulee: a bed of oozy, strongly alkaline mud, down which went a trickle of water — it, too, as we proved, bitterly alkaline and sulphurous. The edges of the lick were packed hard by hooves of its frequenters and covered with their droppings; bighorns, elk, deer, and, we hoped, ibexes had been there. Said Abbot: "All we have to do to get some of 'em is set right here in the edge of the timber and wait for 'em to come."

The others were for going on past the cliff and around the back of the mountain. They left us, and we made ourselves comfortable for, if necessary, a long wait for the game to appear. But the gods were with us. Within an hour some white animals—seven—in single file, came in sight upon the shale east of the cliff, following a trail running quartering to the lick close before us. "Ha! Ibexes, heading straight down toward the lick. Now we were smart to sit here; 'stead of traipsin' on, looking for 'em," Abbot remarked.

"We will have a good look at them, see what they do, before

we shoot," I said.

The trail they followed turned sharply down to avoid a large boulder resting upon the shale and about a hundred yards from us; as they made the turn we got a clear view of them. Like the buffalo, they had humped backs, low hindquarters, chin whiskers, and long, wavy fringes of hair down to the knees of the forelegs, reminding one of a girl's pantalettes in the wind. But there their resemblance to the buffalo ceased, for their heads were long and narrow, their faces dishlike, of mournful, silly expression, and their round, tapering, sharp-pointed horns curved upward and backward instead of outward — deadly scimitars they would be in a fight.

On the seven came, slowly, steadily, and when at the lick, the nearest of them were not twenty yards from us. But that didn't matter as the wind was right. At once they all drank of the little streamlet running down the center of the lick, then turned out to an area where the white mud was about the consistency of semi-hard putty, and, to our great surprise, bit out mouthfuls of it that they deliberately chewed and swallowed. Then, as one after another they drew out from the lick and stood, gazing this way, that way. Abbot nudged me; and quietly, screened by the juniper brush in which we sat, we raised our rifles, sighted them, and each fired once, killing each of us one of the seven. The others instead of running off, merely gave a jump or two and stood vacuously staring at their twitching, dying companions until we arose and started toward them; then with long swift leaps, they took off up the trail and were soon out of our sight.

Before skinning them, we carefully examined our kill, both mature males that would weigh, each of them, all of 250 pounds. We noted that for their size, they had tremendous lung power, that they gave off a strong odor of musk; that underneath their long, coarse hair and next to their skin was a short growth of very fine wool; that at the base of their horns were black, rubbery, wartlike, growths that fairly reeked of musk. "Well, Abbot," I said as we were sharpening our skinning knives, "I have read descriptions of ibexes, seen pictures of them, so I know that our kills, here, are not of that kind, not at all like them except both kinds have four legs, cloven hooves, and both are ruminants.

"Huh! I can tell you what they are," he said. "They're a kind of goat, built a whole lot like the goats I used to see when I was a youngster, away back in Missouri. True, their horns were kind of crinkly, but they had chin whiskers and hair floating out around their knees, same as these here. Yes, sir, they're a kind of goat."

"Well, we'll call them that. Goats they are from now on," I answered. I little thought that I was to learn, two years later, just what the interesting animals were.[1]

We shouldered the hides and a little of the fat meat of our kills and started back down the mountain the way we had come; however, we were not quite done with goats for the day. When passing the east side of the great cliff, we discovered, not far beyond it, a lone goat walking down the steep slope of the mountain and heading toward the top of a small cliff jutting out from the shale. Having arrived at its outer edge, the goat sat down upon its haunches, its hams, its forepart supported by its perpendicular forelegs; with lowered head it gazed at the scene below, sitting just as dogs love to sit and gaze about them. That a ruminant would assume that posture was almost unbelievable. In skinning our kills we had wondered why the fur on their haunches was flattened, matted and soiled. That was now explained; to sit upon their haunches was a habit of the goats. In after years I saw many of them resting and keeping watch upon their surroundings in that posture. They were all males. I doubt the females have that habit.

Abbot and I rested at our wagon for several hours before the others joined us. They arrived loaded with the fat meat of a bighorn ram that Sandoval had killed behind the flat-topped mountain. They said they had seen a number of elk, a band of goats, and three grizzlies, but had not attempted to

---

[1]See *Blackfeet and Buffalo*, page 87.

kill any of them owing to the difficulty of getting out the meat. We had that evening a grand feast of broiled bighorn ribs. Thereafter, for five days we hunted close to camp and having killed all the elk and deer we wanted, struck out for home. Owing to our lack of saddle horses, we had seen but little of the interesting region and had not even visited the upper lakes. I vowed that as soon as possible I would return to explore its valleys and climb its mountains. Well, anyhow, I had given one of its outstanding features a name: Flat Top Mountain.[1]

---

[1]Schultz not only named Flat Top Mountain and Duck Lake on this visit to the St. Mary region, but in later visits bestowed many other names upon its natural features.

To Chief Mountain

The summer was over; the prairie grasses were dried and yellow, the leaves had all fallen from the trees and every morning could be seen a thin scum of ice along the sloughs. We had worked hard all summer and thought we deserved a play spell, so we concluded to spend a week or two at the Chief Mountain lakes. Already the waterfowl were winging their way southward, flock after flock, betokening that winter was close behind them. So we hurriedly got together our outfits, and on the 24th of October pulled out from Kipp & Upham's store on Birch Creek.

There were four of us, Jim, Charlie,[1] myself and an Indian named Man-who-first-took-his-gun-and-ran-ahead, but as this name is a yard or so too long to appear in print more than once we will hereafter call him Scip.

Our outfit consisted of our four-horse team and wagon, one two-horse team and wagon, boat, tent, stove, lantern, bedding and grub—plain grub, such, I think, as the majority of sportsmen would scorn, for it consisted only of bacon, flour, beans, coffee, sugar, potatoes and some sage, summer savory, pepper and salt. We had a big fishing outfit, including a gill-net, for we hoped to catch a barrel of whitefish for winter use.

---

[1]These were Jim Rutherford and Charlie Phemmister, employees of the Indian Agent. They had also participated in the 1883 trip.

Our arsenal comprised four magazine rifles and my 12-bore breechloader. I forbear mentioning the caliber, flatness of trajectory, etc., of the rifles. They are not of the kind recommended by many writers to *Forest and Stream*; but I will give a pointer right here, that more elk, grizzlies, buffalo, bighorn and other game have been killed with guns of our kind than there are left for the men who can shoot only with certain caliber and flatness of trajectory. Come, you who are crying for more powerful and destructive weapons and look over our prairies, scarcely a buffalo is left of the vast herds which used to roam over them. Stroll through our valleys, scarcely a deer is left. Climb our wooded hills and rocky mountains, seldom will you see an elk or bighorn. And yet you want a more destructive weapon! Well, I wish you had one and would begin work by using it on each other, then in future years we might take a day's hunt with fair prospects of getting a piece of meat to take back to camp.

Oct. 24, the first day out, we made only sixteen miles, and camped at the Piegan agency. We noticed a great change in the management here since our last visit. The former agent, Major Young, through false reports to the Indian Department, had caused the rations to be so reduced that a number of the Indians actually starved to death last winter. Among other things he represented that the Indians had over 800 acres of land broken, and were raising plenty of vegetables, wheat, oats, etc. The truth is, they had not forty acres broken, and not half of that was tilled. In the presence of some U.S. Indian Inspectors, other and more serious charges were proven against this reputable member of a Brooklyn Methodist church, but they were not of a character that may appear in print. I visited the lodges on this reservation last winter, where I knew the occupants were dying of hunger. Many, especially the aged, were so weak they could not walk unassisted, and death was plainly visible on their countenances. You will wonder why there was not an outbreak. Well, when Mr. Young first came here he had some trouble with six or seven different Indians, and, singularly, they all died. The cause of their death was at once said to be the agent's wonderful "bad medicine," and so fearful were the rest of this that when he began to starve them they dared not harm him. But for this he would have been killed long ago. Now, however, things are changed. The new agent, Major Allen, is a pleasant, energetic man, interested in the Indians and doing everything in his power to promote their welfare. They now have a fair supply of beef, flour, and other provisions, and are better off than they have been since the buffalo disappeared.

Oct. 25 we made 17 miles, across Badger and Two Medicine Lodge creeks and camped on Cut Bank, which is the north fork of the Marias River. The road was good, over gently rolling prairie. We passed several open lakes which were covered with ducks, but they were very wild and I succeeded in bagging only one, and that a hell-diver, which I cooked and fed to my retriever Babette. We had a good supper though, for while Charlie and I were pitching the tent, Jim caught a fine string of red-throated trout. About dusk I shot a couple of prairie chickens, which I flushed between the tent and the creek.

Oct. 26. — we traveled 18 miles and reached the south fork of Milk River about four o'clock. The road was very rocky and constantly ascending, and the wind blew terribly. An overcoat wasn't a marker, and I could feel it even through the buffalo robe I wrapped around me. The mouth of this river is fully 700 miles from here, and yet here at its source it is larger than it is where it empties into the Missouri. There are no trout in this river nor in any of its tributaries. Just beyond us is Milk River Ridge, the dividing line between the waters of the Arctic and the Atlantic. One more day and we will have crossed it and arrived at our destination. There is no wood here and we take turns feeding the stove with fine willow brush. Time was, only four or five years ago too, when one might have made a good fire here of buffalo chips. Perhaps those certain-caliber-flatness-of-trajectory men will bring them back again. I might have killed a duck or two on the road to-day, but it was too windy to get out of the buffalo robe. The scenery here is bleak but picturesque. All around are flat-topped hills seamed with layers of soft, red sandstone, and here and there are fanciful columns of the same material. To the west, about 20 miles distant, the snow-capped mountains are in plain view.

Why, I would like to know, will civilized people persist in giving places, rivers and mountains such ill-fitting names. The Indian name for this river is *Ke-nuk-tsi-sak-ta*, or little river, which aptly describes it; and the lakes for which we are bound are named *Puh-to-muk-si-kim-iks*, or Inside-big waters, meaning lakes in the mountains.

Oct. 27. — At daybreak we were on the road, and traveled over ridge after ridge, heading for Chief Mountain, which loomed up grandly in the distance. At 3 o'clock we arrived at a large prairie lake, about four miles in length, and as the horses were tired we decided to camp. As soon as we had turned out I took my gun and cartridge bag and went out on a point which reached far out into the lake. The wind was blowing very hard, and the ducks flew high and wild. I shot some twenty odd, but secured only eleven of them. My retriever never having seen any waves before, wouldn't venture in, and I didn't blame her, as it was so cold the spray froze as soon as it struck the rocks. Had a grand supper of stewed duck seasoned with sage and summer savory.

Oct. 28. — Arose at daylight and bagged a few more ducks before breakfast. We were now in the edge of the quaking asps, and confident that we would reach the lake by noon; but alas, we traveled through quaking asp groves, bogs and down timber until 2 o'clock, and then, on arriving at the edge of the hill, found we were about two miles below the lake, so we drove down to the St. Mary's River and camped. While going down Jim, who was ahead, jumped three whitetail, but didn't get a shot. When we came in sight on the hill we noticed an outfit on the other side of the river break camp, hitch up their four-horse team and strike out on the run. There is something suspicious about this. The truth is that last spring some Canadians cut a lot of timber here and drove it down to Fort Macleod, N.W Territory, where they sold it to Sir E.T. Galt's "Coal and Navigation Co." A U.S. deputy marshal was sent here, but the timber was then all across the line, only six miles below here. We suspect that the fellows who left here so suddenly this morning are in the same business.

We are now close to Chief Mountain, which is certainly the grandest mountain I ever saw. It is a great spur jutting out eastward from the main range, and on the top of it is a great mass of rock which gradually tapers until its summit is lost in the clouds. One might ascend to its summit from the west, but the eastern side is a cut bluff thousands of feet high. I should judge that from its base to its summit the mountain is at least 7,000 feet high. St. Mary's River, on which we are camped, is a clear, rapid stream, some seventy-five yards wide, and from the short reach I have seen, I believe that it must contain fish. The ground here and all along the hillside which we came down has been literally torn up by bears; there are no fresh signs, however, and they have probably gone back into the heavy timber to hole up.

Oct. 29. — Our intention was, this morning, to pull out for some good camping place on the lake, but shortly after daylight there came a light skiff of snow. So we all struck out for the quaking asp groves after whitetails. We had not been out long before the sun came out and the snow went off. I returned to camp first, and finding the boys had not come in, started out to catch a mess of trout. Went up the river a little way, and looked down into a clear, deep pool, saw several hundred large fish. Hooked two, but each time lost part of the line, which proved to be rotten. Was returning to camp when I met Jim coming back, followed by a four-horse team load of people, who proved to be an outfit from the agency, here for a little sport. They were Mr. Fowler, Mr. Bird, Oliver, the interpreter,[1] and two small boys. These last made themselves conspicuous by shooting their repeating rifles constantly and in every direction, regardless of the lives of the rest of the party. Charlie and the Indian having now returned, the latter with the saddle of a fine buck, we hitched up and all drove up the lake a mile or so and camped by a bay on the south side. Immediately we had the tents up, we

[1]Oliver was Oliver Sandoval, son of an old Spanish employee of the American Fur Company. Fowler and Bird were not otherwise identified.

pitched the boat, and although it was nearly dark, Jim and Mr. Fowler went out and caught three lake trout, the largest of which weighed about twelve pounds. These trout are identical with those found in the Fulton Chain and other lakes of the Adirondacks.

The lower St. Mary's Lake is about seven miles long and, in places, a mile wide. On the west side of the lake an immense flat-topped mountain comes down to the water's edge, and on the east side rises a high, steep ridge—it would be called a mountain in the East—thickly wooded with fir. From this ridge one can get glimpses of the upper lake, much larger than this one and walled in by stupendous mountains. Beyond rise peak after peak of jagged mountains, some of them with sheer cliffs thousands of feet high.

Oct. 30. — This morning Mr. Bird, Oliver and Jim started out after bighorn and Mr. Fowler and I went fishing. We first tried a spoon, and trolled in deep and shallow water with and without lead, but didn't get a strike. We then tried hand lines baited with meat, and in a few minutes Mr. Fowler caught four large ones, the largest of which would have weighed ten pounds. I hooked a large one, but he broke away before I could gaff him. In the afternoon Mr. Fowler went out alone and fished with two lines. He was playing a fish when he saw his other line go spinning through the water. This last fish proved to be an immense fellow, fully four feet long, Mr. Fowler said, but alas! the gaff broke and the monster still lives. About 8 o'clock the Indian and the two small boys returned from down the river with thirteen trout (red-throated), the largest I ever saw; none of them would have weighed less than two pounds, and some, I have no doubt, would have tipped the scales at four. Saw a mallard in the bay, flushed it and brought it down. Babette retrieved it and laid it at my feet, when it took wing again; brought it down with the left barrel, this time dead. Just before supper Mr. Fowler went out behind the camp, and in a few minutes bagged six grouse and two mountain rabbits — fattest grouse I ever saw.

At dark the hunters returned. They saw plenty of sheep

and mortally wounded two, which went up a cliff where they could not be followed. They report plenty of elk, bear and deer sign. The country is very rough, and way up in the mountains they found three large lakes which are the source of Swift Current, a creek which empties into the river about a mile below the lake on the north side.

Oct. 31. — This morning the Agency party left for home. They took with them fifty fine lake and red-throated trout; the largest of each kind would have weighed about twenty-five and five pounds respectively. Took a spin on the lake with Charlie and caught several large lakers. If "Kingfisher" were here I believe he would for once get all the big fish and spring water he wanted. There are probably fifty springs for each mile of lake shore, and lake trout are so large and plenty that it is no pleasure to fish.

After dark a flock of geese lit on the shore near camp and I managed to get one of them. Crossed the lake near the outlet to-day, and as we suspected, found that the party which pulled out so suddenly had been at work in the timber. We found several thousand fine logs which they had cut. It seems to me that in the great and glorious province of Alberta, Dominion of Canada, these men could find enough timber without coming over here and stealing it from us.

As we were about to return to camp we saw two four-horse outfits rolling in, and were agreeably surprised to find that one of them belonged to Ben S. who is on a prospecting trip with two young men named Dick and John. The other was our friend M., a beaver trapper by trade and known to all by the name of Medicine Beaver. They crossed the outlet of the lake, and we packed up and all together moved up near the head of the lake, where we made a good camp. We had been using our gill net below with poor success; here, however, we did a little better, and during our stay at the lake managed to catch, in all, ninety-four whitefish, which, when weighed on our return home, tipped the scales at 232 pounds. I am satisfied that whitefish are very plenty here. Our nets were too fine, and only four feet deep, and the lake trout completely ruined them by tearing holes in them the size of a barrel.

In the inlet we caught another variety of trout. It is very long and thin and has an immense mouth, and is colored more like the Eastern brook trout; the belly is white, it lacks the red throat of the other variety, and has large dull crimson spots on its sides. The red-throated trout here are very small mouthed, and are shaped very like the bass, they are so plenty that the most insatiable "trout hog" would here become tired of the sport.

Nov. 2. — A camp of North Piegans, under Chief Yellow Fish,[1] came in to-day and moved up to the foot of the upper lake. They say that they are starved out at their agency at Fort Macleod, Northwest Territory, and are here after game. This is an unlucky thing for us, not on account of what they will kill, but because they will scare everything out of the country. An Indian is insatiable. When he sees a band of game he is not satisfied with making one killing, but will keep following it and shooting as long as possible. This gives the game a tremendous scare, and they get out of the country as soon as possible. By the way, this will be a good place for the certain caliber flatness-of-trajectory men. They can sit on the lake shore and with telescopes on their improved rifles, kill sheep and goats on the top of the mountain. Afterward they can send their guides up after the choice portions of meat. We hear grouse drumming every night; had thought that their drumming season was the spring only.

Nov. 5. — Ben, Jim and the Medicine Beaver went up Swift Current to-day, sheep hunting. I took a short stroll through the brush and killed eight grouse. It is really no sport to hunt grouse here; as soon as one is flushed it lights on the nearest twig and will allow one to approach within ten feet of it. Wing-shooting is impossible, and the only thing is to walk up and blow off their heads.

Ben's two young men have been sinking holes in many likely places, but as yet have been unable to get to bed-rock

---

[1]This was not the same Indian who accompanied Schultz in September, 1885 on Grinnell's first visit to the St. Mary region. That Indian was a French half-blood.

on account of water. It is no boy's play to "delve for gold."

Nov. 6. — The sheep hunters returned this evening with three fine bucks, the fattest animals I ever saw. They went up Swift Current and passed five lakes, the two last of which are on the very top of the mountains. The last one has a sheer fall at the outlet of 200 feet. They say the scenery is grand, sheep plenty and the lakes teem with fish. Every evening now the boys congregate in our tent and tell stories "until further notice." Jim told us an amusing experience of his this evening. Long ago he and a partner were prospecting on the head waters of the Yellowstone. One day they saw a grizzly, and his partner shot it, wounding it slightly. The bear ran in Jim's direction, and Jim, badly scared, made for a tree and thought he climbed it, but when the bear had passed he found himself sitting at the base, his arms fast locked around the trunk.

One day Ben, Jim, Medicine Beaver and I concluded to go sheep hunting. We took saddle horses and one pack animal, a little bacon, bread and coffee, bedding and axe, and started for the head of the upper lake. We crossed the inlet above, where Yellow Fish was camped. The Indians told us that sheep were very plenty, and the numerous goat and sheep hides pegged out around the camp bore witness that for once they told the truth.

Leaving their camp we came to an old Kootenai trail, which we were told reached across the range into Missoula.[1] This we followed through dense quaking asp groves, thickets of pine, and down timber, and after about two hours' ride came to a long park pretty well up on the side of the mountain. Although the view from here was magnificent we had no eye for it, but kept our necks craned toward the rocks above us in hopes of seeing a band of sheep. Riding through this park we came to an immense limestone ledge, which reached from the mountain above to the water's edge, ter-

---

[1] Presumably over Gunsight Pass.

minating in a cut bluff. Running up the nearly perpendicular side of this ledge is an old elk trail, and we could see that
the Indians had gone over it with their horses, but we
thought it too risky a place for our animals, and turning
them loose we pitched a camp in a grove of balsams at the
foot of the ledge and about fifty yards from the lake. As soon
as we had eaten supper and made down a thick bed of balsam
boughs, we found night had come, and after sitting around
the fire for an hour or two, turned in. Now, we hadn't been in
bed very long before an owl perched in a tree top close by, and
said very plainly, "Go way! Go way! Go way!" At least this is
the way Medicine Beaver interpreted its speech, and further,
he assured us that we would kill no sheep on this trip as the
owls scolding us was a sure sign that we were out of luck.
Some time in the night Ben and the trapper assured us I said
in a plain voice, "Throw it away," and Jim, sleeping by my
side, said as plainly, "Yes, throw it away, it's no account
anyhow."

As morning approached I arose and built a fire, and after a
hasty and frugal breakfast we climbed the ledge on the old
elk trail and reached the top of it at daylight. From here a
long high mountain extended to the upper end of the lake.
Jim and I concluded to follow it on the lake side and Ben and
the Beaver were to go round it and meet us at the further
end. After a long hard climb Jim and I got above the timber
and found a very fair sheep trail which ran along the side of
the mountains close up under the "reefs" or perpendicular
rock walls, which are a distinctive feature of these mountains. Almost every mountain I have seen in this country is
capped with these rock walls, some of which run up to a great
height, gradually narrowing, so that the top is apparently as
sharp as a jack-knife. Here on every side of us, and indeed
along the whole length of the mountain we saw plenty of
fresh sheep signs, but all that day we never saw a sheep, the
Indians had apparently scared out of the country those they
had not killed. We kept following the trail higher and
higher, further and further until we came to what Jim called
the "jumping off place," for here our mountains ended ab-

ruptly in a cañon of great depth. Here we were well repaid for our arduous climb. Never in my life did I behold such grand scenery. Below us several thousand feet, lay the lake (about twelve miles long), its unruffled surface dotted with several small islands. In places the lake is very narrow, some of them apparently not 200 yards wide. I could not describe it better than to say that it is an immense cañon partly filled with water. Save at the head and foot of the lake there is no shore; from the very edge the water has that dark green hue which betokens great depth.

On the opposite side, and on our side of the lake across the cañon, the mountains rise to a great height, some of them shaped like a saddle. Beyond the head of the lake is a long, wide, densely timbered valley, and on the upper left-hand side of this valley is a mountain, the top of which is a true glacier.[1] With the glasses it appeared to be at least 300 feet thick. We could see large fissures in it, and in one place a large mass had apparently lately broken off. A large stream of water which comes from this glacier dashes over a perpendicular cut on the face of the mountain at least 250 feet in height. We were unable to determine the length of the glacier, as intervening mountains obstructed a view of either end.

After resting here for an hour or two, and Ben and the trapper failing to put in an appearance we started back toward camp. I was surprised to see large flocks of geese flying above us, above the tops of the highest mountains, and apparently heading for the other side of the mountains. I always supposed that waterfowl fly north and south — that those which breed north of here winter in Southern Utah, Arizona and New Mexico. Is it possible that the destination of these was the Pacific slope?

About half way back to camp we stopped beside a little stream, which gushed out of a reef just above us, to rest and wet our whistles. As we sat there Jim, who is one of "ye ancient prospectors," picked up several pieces of float quartz,

---

[1]Blackfoot Glacier

which were rich with gold and silver. As we were near the top of the mountain the lead from which they came could not have been far off, but as we were tired, and as this country is an Indian reservation, we concluded we didn't want a gold mine, and started on to camp, which we reached without further adventure. Ben and the trapper had not returned, there was not enough grub to last us till morning, so we saddled up and started home, leaving a note to this effect, stuck up by the only remaining piece of bread. The moon evidently isn't right for sheep, at least we didn't see any, and as this is the last piece of bread we have, decided to light out.

We hadn't been in camp long and had just finished our supper, when Ben and the trapper came. When they left us in the morning they got around behind the mountain, came to a lake high up and completely walled in by cut bluffs, and saw seven goats on the other side of it, but had not time to approach them. Thoroughly disgusted they fired their guns and had the satisfaction of seeing the goats strike out on the run, heading for Missoula,[1] where Yellow Fish and his band of hunters will have to follow them if they want their hides.

We put in, altogether, twenty-one days at the lake, hunting and fishing, the others trapping and prospecting — to me, twenty-one days brim full of pleasure. At last the weather turned cold, and the snow came down thick and fast.

"Boys," said Jim, "the moon isn't right."
Myself — "Fish in the lakes."
The trapper — "Beaver in their holes."
Charlie — "Sheep high up."
Ben — "Bed rock deep."
Dick — "White-tail scarce."
John — "Goose gone over, and let's go too."

So we decided then and there to break camp the next day. We had concluded the night before to make the next camp on the South Fork of Milk River, but the hill, where we climbed it, was much steeper than we thought it would be, and it took

---

[1]Presumably over Cut Bank pass.

us all day to get up, pulling up one wagon at a time with ten horses.

At the South Fork we camped two days and hunted. Jim and I rode up to the mountains after sheep. As we were riding along we came across a fresh sheep trail in the snow and saw the band just beyond going down into a pocket or basin on the side of the mountain. I ran to the right and Jim to the left. Ere long the band appeared beyond Jim going up the side of the mountain. Jim killed one, a fat doe. They were a long way from me and I failed to hit.

Nov. 21 — We arrived at the North Fork of Cut Bank. There is a good trail[1] which reaches over the mountains into Missoula and is much traveled by the several tribes of mountain Indians. The trail apparently follows up Cut Bank to its source. As far up as we went we found a wide, densely-timbered cañon, walled in by tremendous mountains. Old game signs were very plenty here, but there had been no cold weather and snow to drive the elk down, so we contented ourselves with hunting deer, and killed four altogether.

Nov. 23 — We drove down to the junction of the North and South Forks, and on the 24th reached the agency.

All in all, we had a pleasant trip, plenty of fish and game for camp use, and, above all, a sojourn among the pines and lakes so like those of our boyhood days.[2] As a resort for sportsmen the Chief Mountain country cannot be excelled. The scenery is grand, game plenty, the fishing unexcelled. Here the angler will find new ground, lakes and streams on whose bosoms a fly has never been cast, and in whose crystal depths a bait has never been dropped.

Upper Marias River, M.T., January 1885

---

[1]Over Cut Bank pass.

[2]Referring to the Adirondack region of upper New York.

White Goats and Bull Trout

Little did I think that my ineffective pen would record the events of our autumn hunt. I had expected that "Yo"[1] would, as usual, be the scribe, and in his bright and entertaining way, relate our adventures on lake and mountain, and faithfully portray the beauties of the Upper Lake. Business matters, however, prevented him joining our party. I shall not give a record of each day's events, for we were at the Lakes[2] over a month; and some days had no events, while an account of those that did would fill a volumn of no mean proportions. My main object is to tell you something about the white goat and the "bull trout."

There were in our party three gentlemen from England—the Colonel and the Governor,[3] aged 51 and 49 years, and Cecil,[4] a young man of four and twenty. Then there was Jack Bean, from the Yellowstone, Joe Kipp, with a cook, a herder, and the writer, eight persons all told. Our outfit comprised a four-horse team and wagon, a number of saddle horses, tents, stove, and all the grub and duffle necessary for such a trip.

---

[1]Pseudonym of George Bird Grinnell.
[2]St. Mary lakes.
[3]Members of the Baring family of English bankers.
[4]Cecil Baring was a nephew, manager of the family's New York branch.

The 9th of September we arrived at the foot of the Lower Lake. The Colonel and the Governor had their fly-rods jointed in no time, and while we were putting up the tents and getting things in order they went to the outlet and caught a string of trout for supper, all red-throated trout (*Salmo purpuratus*) and none over 2 ½ lbs. weight. After supper a council of war was held, and it was decided that the first trip should be made up Swift Current.

By noon of the next day we had the horses packed and were on the way, leaving the cook behind to watch the main camp and take care of the spare horses. It was a windy day, and dark clouds enveloped the mountain tops. But then such was to be expected. I never yet went up Swift Current without having to face a driving wind, accompanied by rain or snow. "Yo," in his "Walled-In Lakes" papers last year fully described the grand and rugged scenery along this valley. We saw lots of bear and some elk sign along the trail, and Cecil shot a couple of dusky grouse. When we were within half a mile of the camping ground it began to snow, and right glad we were to reach the shelter of the pines. The tent was soon up, and in spite of the storm the Governor caught a number of trout, none very large, but all as fat and firm fleshed as fish could be. As night drew on how cheering was the warm, dry tent. Having partaken of a generous supper, we lay back on our beds and smoked, and were at peace. Without the wind soughed through the pines and shrieked past the crags above, the hail rattled down on the roof, and the roar of the waterfall near by joined in, making withal a combination of sound pleasant to the ear, and so soothing that some of us fell asleep ere the pipes were half burned out.

The next morning the first thing that met my eyes as I stepped out was a band of goats near the top of the wall-faced mountain, just where "Yo" and I saw some last year. "Goats in sight," I cried out, and such a flinging of blankets and hurried scrambling from fur bags you never saw. No need for any one to ask where, for we were camped almost at the base of the mountain, and one looking up the sheer wall couldn't help seeing the white animals so sharply outlined against the black slate rock. They were probably 1,500 yds. above us. Glasses were brought out, and every one took a long look at them. In a short time breakfast was ready, and during the meal it was decided that Jack should go behind the mountain and then climb to the top. We could see with the glasses that the mountain was quite broken at the top and from the point where the goats were sloped back a little, and we hoped that Jack would be able to get down to them. That he could not see the animals until right on them we well knew, so a system of signals was arranged to guide him in his movements. After Jack had gone, the Colonel and Governor got out their fly-rods and fished below the falls for an hour or more, but didn't get a single bite, although they tried several kinds of flies. The rest loitered around camp and watched the goats. They didn't move about much, and after a while some of them lay down, at least we thought they did, for they suddenly disappeared.

After a long time Jack came in sight on top of the mountain, and to the left of the goats. We signaled him to move down and to his left. We soon saw that it was dangerous work, for he moved very slowly and often went up back and tried another place. After an hour or more, aided by our signals, he succeeded in getting over the goats, and apparently not over 75 yards above them. Soon we saw the smoke of his gun and then heard the report. Not a goat moved. Again and again he fired. Yet the animals heeded not. We concluded that he was shooting at a goat we could not see. After a while we saw him turn and ascend, sometimes crawling, and again going up hand over hand, and we watched him until he reached the top and disappeared from view.

As we were sitting down to the evening meal, the hunter appeared and told us the result of his climb. Guided by our signals he had got down to where we saw him shoot, but further he could not go without a pair of wings. He had seen no goats, but fired hoping to scare them out where he could see them. Having thus briefly described his adventures, he fell to, and ate such a heavy supper as only a man can after climbing mountains all day.

During the night the wind again came roaring down the valley, and the morning broke dark and chilly. Away down on the St. Mary's we could see clear sky and the sun shining brightly on the hills beyond the lake. So we decided to leave this gloomy and unlucky place for easier hunting grounds and a more congenial climate. The goats were still in sight, near where we had seen them the previous day, and after breakfast the rifles were got out and we tried to scare them away. The English gentlemen had 110-grain express rifles, double-barrel, and the rest of us were armed with big Winchesters, except Joe, who had a "'73 model" carbine, a relic of buffalo-running days. For some time we kept up a lively fusilade at all elevations but we couldn't see the bullets strike and the goats never even stopped feeding. We soon packed up and left the place in disgust, yet had we stayed a day to two longer we would have got game, for there were other mountains beyond, and on the opposite side of the valley apparently easy to climb, and that there are plenty of goats is beyond a doubt. I made up my mind to try it again some time and explore the upper part of the valley, which I am sure has never been visited by a white man, and seldom if ever by a redskin.

With a feeling of relief we left the gloomy valley and emerged into the sunshine at St. Mary's. After supper the Colonel and Governor once more tried the fishing, and with good success, for during the few moments they had before dark they caught more than enough for breakfast. Again the council was called, and it was decided that we move camp to the foot of the Upper Lake, and the boats be got in readiness for an exploration of the unknown country beyond. The "Yo" boat was already there. We had a canvas affair in the wagon, brought all the way from London, and the old scow was at the head of the Lower Lake. Early the next morning all the duffle was stowed on the wagon, the horses hitched up, and we started. The distance was only nine or ten miles, and in a few hours we were comfortably settled in camp at the foot of the lake close by the outlet. As the creek leaves the lake it flows very swiftly for about twenty-five yards, and then forms a deep, wide pool. Here, after dinner, rods were jointed and we proceeded to fish. The first trout was taken by the Governor. It was a *Salmo purpuratus* and weighed 3½ lbs. Quite a number of these fish were taken. Down deep in the water I could see quite a number of large fish. Some, I knew, were lake trout, and others I surmised were "bull trout." The flies we had were very small, so I rigged a large hook for the Governor and baited it with a generous slice from a trout's belly. This he used exactly as one would a fly. At the second cast there was a tremendous splurge. A large fish rose clear from the water and took the hook with him as he went down. The Governor struck at the proper time, and now the fun began. You all know how it is: "merry *whirr* of the reel," "line hissing through the water," "rod bent nearly double," etc. The fish made a gallant fight and in due time was brought to the landing net. It proved to be, as I thought, a "bull trout," and weighed 7½ lbs. In shape these fish are long and slender, the head is long and pointed and the mouth large. The color of the back is like that of *Salmo fontinalis*. The belly is generally a golden yellow, sometimes yellowish white, and the sides are dotted with faint red and yellow spots. It is, I suppose, an Arctic trout, but whether it has been identified I know not. After this we caught here as many of these trout as of the red-throated ones, and once in a while a laker was taken, just for a change. They average about 5 lbs. in weight, but I have seen several which I dare say would weigh more than 15 lbs. I have never seen one which weighed less than 3 lbs. As a game fish they cannot be excelled by any other trout I have ever seen, nor by the bass. They are desperate fighters, and like the salmon, break water many times before they are enveloped in the landing net. I have never caught them except in the fall, and have never found any eggs or milt in them. I conclude, therefore, that they are spring spawners. Seldom, too, have I found anything in their stomachs, though the fish were always in good condition. What a puzzling study is the distribution of fish. Here in these lakes the tribe is represented by species from the Mississippi water shed, from the Great Lakes and the Arctic, as follows:

Mississippi waters: The cusk (*Lota maculosa*) and the red-throated trout (*Enox nobilior*), lake trout, (*Salmo namayeush*), and whitefish (*Coregonus wilsonii*). Arctic waters: Bull trout (*Salvelinus malma*). The Maskinonje, however, are very rare. In all my fishing here, I never caught but two, which weighed respectively 12 and 16 lbs. I think the water is too cold for them to thrive. White-fish are also found in many lakes and rivers of the Arctic watershed.

J.W. Shultz
Montana

THE AMERICAN SPORTSMAN'S JOURNAL.

NEW YORK, THURSDAY, OCTOBER 14, 1880.

CONTENTS.

FOREST AND STREAM

NEW YORK, THURSDAY, OCTOBER 14, 1880.

VELOCITY OF SHOT.—We promised some weeks ago the publication of the full text of Prof. Mayer's paper on the Velocity of Shot. We regret to state that, owing to the serious illness of Prof. Mayer, he has been unable to prepare the manuscript for our columns, but promises it to the readers of the FOREST AND STREAM at early as practicable. An imperfect synopsis of the article appeared, at the time it was read, in some of the daily papers, and has since been copied by some of our exchanges. We thought it due to Prof. Mayer and to our readers to publish the article, when we do publish it, complete and as its author would have it appear.

SPORTSMEN'S ASSOCIATIONS OF WESTERN PENNSYLVANIA.—The Sportsmen's Association of Western Pennsylvania has 300 members; in fact, 362 appeared at last roll call. The association is now ten years old, and still growing. It is composed mainly of business and professional men, who have done much to enforce the game laws. Their club room is 50 feet front by 80 feet deep, situated in the most populous part of Pittsburg. The first floor is divided into a reading room, library, card room and a large billiard room. The second story is called the assembly or meeting room, and besides the numerous chairs and tables for officers and members, contains cases of rare specimens of trees of the sportsmen's Association, as well as a large variety of small birds purchased from a skilful taxidermist in Massachusetts, making in all about 3,000 good specimens. Their exhibit of animals and reptiles is quite small, and some of the boys had better go after snakes a little.

The Alleghany Sportsmen's Association of Allegheny county is a little over one year old, and has at least 100 members, with headquarters in Allegheny City.

A NEWSPAPER'S RESPONSIBILITIES.

AS newspapers are managed by individuals they are no less liable to error than the latter. And, although employing the impersonal "we," their responsibilities to the public to their readers and advertisers are no less binding than are those of the individual business man. Moreover, because of their greater facilities for obtaining information, there are certain duties incumbent on the publishers of a newspaper from which commercial men are free. They must especially avoid advertising any article or implement that may be injurious to health or dangerous to life or limb. No concern can shirk the responsibility which will attach to it if it knowingly advertises a dangerous gun or an unsalable pistol. Every one knows that a safe rifle cannot be made for $5, and if proven represent that they are selling such a gun for that sum, this representation in prima facie evidence that the gun is not a proper arm to put into the hands of the shooting fraternity.

But a newspaper is not bound to furnish brains for its readers. It must exercise due care in receiving advertisements and in this respect must protect itself and its patrons. It cannot, however, vouch for the honesty or business standing of all those who advertise goods for sale in its columns. Its readers, in treating with strangers who hire at a distance, must be governed by the ordinary and generally accepted rules of business. A capitalist in Boston does not buy a mine from a Colorado prospector without taking some measures to see that the property in which he is to put his money is really what it is represented to be. Why should a sportsman in Texas buy a dog from a breeder in Maine without inquiring as to the responsibility and trust-worthiness of the seller? Every man who shoots has his own ideas as to what a dog should do and be, and scarcely any two men think alike on this subject; moreover, as few men understand how to handle a dog, therefore an animal which will work well before a good handler may be worse than useless to another man, whose experience or knack is less. Years ago we laid down for our selves a rule from which we have never deviated. It was simply this: never to buy a horse, dog, or gun without ourselves giving it a fair trial. We are willing to pay the expense charges both ways, and to deposit the price agreed on with some reliable party, preferably the Express Company. If at the end of the time agreed on the dog does not give satisfaction it is returned, and the only loss we have suffered is that of the charges.

We sometimes receive complaints from persons who have bought dogs through advertisements in our columns, which do not satisfy them. Such persons are often themselves to blame for the haste that they have incurred. They have not taken proper precautions to guard themselves against loss and bad treatment on the part of designing men. In these days of express companies no man need part with his money before he sees the goods which he is buying.

Another point to which attention must be called, is the of ges which occasionally appear to give something of great value for little or nothing. It would scarcely appear necessary to warn intelligent men against offers of this kind, but certainly that "fools are not all dead yet," and each one who sends his money thinks that he will escape being swindled and that the rest of the community will come to grief. We have little charity for the people who are gulled by these transparent humbugs. They need a lesson of this kind. It's all who are tempted in this way, we would say, however, beware of a three-cent stamp, or will agree that to shall have free advertising in Forest and Stream, so that the sports men of America may all avail themselves of the opportunity offered.

In considering the advertisements offered us, we try to exclude all those which have anything about them which appears suspicious, but occasionally, through misrepresentation or from some inadvertence advertisements may appear which should not have been admitted to our columns.

FOREST AND STREAM cannot answer to be responsible for casual advertisers or its columns or for those replying to such advertisements. We recommend our patrons, whether reading our advertisers, in doing business with strangers, to demand references to have goods sent by express C.O.D., and in fact to protect themselves by all legitimate means. No one in these days expects a customer to buy goods, without inspecting them, and no one need feel aggrieved at having an intending purchaser use reasonable business precautions in business dealings. Of course, with a majority of our advertisers such precautions are unnecessary. The statements of established houses which have a standing in the commercial world may be implicitly trusted.

"SEALED CANS."

THIRTY-FIVE years ago, Sir John Franklin, with a company of one hundred and thirty-five men, sailed from England to attempt a northwest passage to the Pacific Ocean.

No survivor of that party ever returned. The mystery surrounding the fate of the expedition has never been dispelled. In the melancholy interest with which the civilized world has not yet ceased to regard it, the Franklin expedition stands alone. It is the great tragedy of the Sea is Land.

Attention has been newly called to the subject by the search expedition of Lieutenant Schwatka, who claims to have discovered in King William's Land relics of the Franklin expedition, and some of the viable dispatches received from England during the past weeks commenting upon these alleged discoveries are of the most startling and unexpected character.

Commander Cheyne, who was attached to one of the former search expeditions, charges that Franklin's men perished, not from Arctic exposure, but from starvation; in short, not to put too fine a point upon it, that they were murdered by the contractor who furnished the canned means for the expedition. The cans labeled "mutton" and "beef" contained, it is alleged, nothing but bones and offal. And when the official inquest is held upon the skeleton of one of the Franklin party, which is now on its way to England, Commander Cheyne says that he will reiterate and prove his charges against this contractor.

This, it must be confessed, takes away all the poetry from the Franklin expedition. If these terrible charges of Commander Cheyne can be proven, or if there is ground for even a suspicion that they may be true, the sympathy of the world for the victims will straightway be turned into indignation against the contractor.

The moral of all this is of more application than the North Pole.

Every man who seals a tin can, affixing his own signature to assure its genuineness, and then, prompted by his untamed greed for gain, and knowing full well that the possible consequences of his deception may cost human life, deliberately affixes that that can contains one thing, when he knows it to contain another thing, assumes in so doing a tremendous and awful responsibility.

It matters little whether the deception accomplishes its disastrous result among the green fields sought for pleasure, or amid the wastes of an Arctic land; it is of little moment whether the true nature of the contents of that can be discovered at once or five or thirty-five years afterward.

PEMMO. It was once the custom when public offices had proved unfaithful to their trust, to punish them from their native land; in these days a happier custom prevails, whereby a term of cheerful exile is made a stepping stone to all varied rank. The Forest and Stream promise this best compliments to Commander L. A. Beardslee, late of the U. S. Jamestown, stationed at Sitka, Alaska, and now detached and on his way home to be examined for promotion. Commander Beardslee's task at Sitka was one of some magnitude, the governing of a mixed population, made up of diverse nationalities and for the most part not accustomed to government of any kind. Something of the nature of this

White Goat Hunting

The scow having been hauled up from the lower lake, and the canvas boat put in the water, we were all ready to begin our explorations of the upper country. So one bright morning, leaving the cook and herder to watch the main camp and horses, we started out with a stiff ash breeze in our favor. The lake was perfectly quiet, and the boats, especially the canvas affair, were heavily loaded, so we hurried along, hoping to get to the head of the lake before the wind rose. For about six miles the lake is quite wide, perhaps 1½ miles at the broadest place. On the southside is the great pine-covered ridge which divides the Arctic and Atlantic waters. On the north old Singleshot looms up, a wonderful maze of rock, bright and beautiful now in the sunshine, far different from when "Yo"[1] and I groped along its side in the dense fog. We kept close to the north shore going up, as it was the shortest route, and made the narrows in about an hour and a half. Here the steep mountains rise on each side, and the narrows are two great ledges of rock which jut far out into the water. In places they are perpendicular and several hundred feet high. Old Time has worn great holes in them at the water's edge, and as we passed along the rising waves surged into them with a melancholy roar. It made one shudder to think of an upset there. The water is inky black, a sign of great depth, and along the slippery ledge is no crevice or foothold. Passing through, we found that the lake widened rapidly to a breadth of about two miles. On the south shore, commencing

[1]Pseudonym used by George Bird Grinnell.

96

at the narrows, is a series of mountains, rising ever higher and higher, until they join the summit at the head of the valley. Between each mountain or peak is a basin, often walled by ice, from which a small stream comes tumbling down into the lake. On the north shore, separated from Singleshot by a deep and narrow cañon, is a long, high red rock mountain which reaches nearly to the head of the lake. It is crowned by pillars and fantastic groups of time-worn rock of great height. This is the "Goat Mountain," where "Yo"[1] and I one day attempted to hunt in the rain and fog.

The water was getting pretty rough, and after a further pull of about two miles we landed in a little cove to rest and eat our lunch. Opposite this point, quite a distance from shore, is a small, rocky island, on which grow a few wind-bent pines and quaking asps. I have named it *Nat-os-ap-i* Island, after a chief whose spirit has long since gone to the "sandhills." The meaning is Sun-old-man, and although it is a queer name for an island, it is at least original and much better than stony island, pine island, stormy island or any such common name. We resumed the oars, still hugging the north shore, and about three miles from where we ate our lunch on a low point in a grove of tall pines made camp. On the far end of this point a glacier stream flows swiftly into the lake, its milk-colored water making a vivid contrast with the clear green waters of the lake.

While getting camp in shape the elder gentlemen had jointed their fly-rods, and now came a shout for landing nets. Rushing out we found a fisherman on each side of the stream where it empties into the lake. Both rods were bent, and the lines cutting through the water at a great rate. The trout were gamy and fought long and valiantly. When brought to the net they weighed respectively 2½ and 3¼ lbs. The next fish, caught by the Governor, weighed 4½ lbs. While we were admiring this the Colonel struck one. It made for deep water and played back and fourth for what seemed to us an interminable time. However, he was finally landed and weighed, and pulled down the scales to 5 lbs. plump. We had two sets of

---

[1]Pseudonym used by George Bird Grinnell.

scales and both registered the fish at 5 lbs. plump. This was the largest *Salmo purpuratus* caught on the trip, and in fact the largest one of the kind I ever saw. If any reader knows of a larger one, will he kindly mention it in *Forest and Stream*? Several other fish were caught, none under 2 lbs. or over 3½ lbs. weight. During our stay here we often whiled away a spare hour catching lake trout. Standing on the shore and fishing with bait or spoon one could catch as many as one wanted. They did not average so large as those caught at the foot of the lake, the largest weighing only 7 lbs.

Next morning Cecil and I seemed to be the only ones who cared to hunt. So after breakfast, we shouldered our guns and struck out. The glacier and the next one to the west, which, on account of its great height, I have named *Nat-o-ye-tup-po* – Going-to-the-Sun. Following up this stream for a mile or more, we came to a very steep hill of slate rock, through which the creek had cut a narrow channel. We could see up it about 100 yards to where it made a bend to the left. From top to bottom this part of the cañon is about 200 feet in depth, and of an even width of about 4 feet. We would have tried to go through it had it not been for several little falls, where we would have been sure to get wet. Lucky for us that we did not make the attempt for half a mile further on we couldn't see the creek. Here the top of the cañon is about 30 yds. across, and the steep sides are so slippery with dead pine needles that we did not dare attempt to look down into it. It must, however, be very deep, for we could hear the faint roar of a waterfall, which sounded as if it were way down in the bowels of the earth. A mile further we emerged from the pines and found ourselves at the entrance of a big round basin hemmed in by mountains of great height, some of which are perpendicular walls of rock rising far into the sky. On the west side of the basin, high up, are several glaciers, from which flow good-sized streams, but falling from such great heights and broken by several ledges, they are lost in spray before reaching the bottom. In the basin and on the less steep sides of the mountains stunted pines and beds of juniper grow in profusion. All in all, it is one of the grandest places I ever saw.

We had made a hearty breakfast and felt like climbing, so we went half way up the basin and started to climb on the right, the easiest place we could see. We had no dangerous places, but it was very steep, and we were four hours in reaching the summit. We had seen, half way up, many fresh goat signs, but here on top was not a single track, old or new, save three fresh trails in the snow, made by a mountain lion, and her young. Except for the beautiful basin below, it was a dreary view from this elevated position. The Goat Mountain shut out all sight of the prairie, and of the valley of the lake. Looking the other way, was nothing but peak after peak of bare rock, ice and snow. Yet the scene was not without value. It gave one an idea—so far as man can comprehend such an idea—of the great force which was required to upheave these masses from the level plain.

We ate our lunch up here and for drink ate snow. Then becoming chilly, we went along a little further, and finding a shale slide which reached clear to the foot of the basin, we started down, and running, sliding and jumping, soon reached the bottom. Down by the creek we found some huckleberry bushes fairly loaded with fruit, and were feasting on them, when happening to look up, I saw a big goat, nearly opposite us feeding. He was at the foot of the rock wall, just at the edge of the shale, half a mile away. Between, the shale sloped at an angle of 50 degrees, and as it was a very old slide, covered in places with grass, stunted pines and bunches of juniper, it afforded excellent shelter for us to creep up to him. Just as we were about to start for him there was a roar and crash which fairly shook the mountain. Such an awful, deafening roar I have never before heard. A large mass of ice, tons and tons of it, had broken from a glacier far up on the mountain side, and shivered into fine fragments, was pouring over the wall, glistening and scintillating in the sunshine like diamonds. Down, down it came, and falling into a branch of the stream, was soon sweeping by us, a tinkling, seething mass. All this roar and confusion of sound had not disturbed the goat any; he was still quietly feeding, as if with him this was an every day sight. As soon as the ice had all passed we crossed the creek and began to climb. We got along all right until within 250 yds. of the animal, when he smelled us, and sitting down on his haunches like a dog, head down, he proceeded to scrutinize the valley. Cecil now went alone, and got within 150 yds. of him. The climbing was very steep, and before Cecil could regain his breath, the goat started to walk along. Cecil fired both barrels at him, one after the other. The goat stopped, looked around and then resumed his walk. Twice more the rifle spoke, and this time one of the bullets struck near the animal and it started to climb. Going up a piece he struck a narrow shelf and ran along this faster and faster, for Cecil's bullets were flying around him pretty lively. Now the animal stopped. Before him was a very steep and dangerous place, for the spray from a glacier made the rocks very slippery. The goat turned back. Should he come toward us a hundred yards, there was a place where he could ascend the mountain and soon get out of sight. Then I began to fire, too. Three times the goat ran back and forth, stopped each time by the bullets striking before him. The third time back he made some desperate leaps, crossed the slippery place, ascended a few yards, made two last mighty leaps, and stopped on a small shelf not much longer than his body. Above, beyond, below was the sheer rock wall. He could go no further. The little ledge afforded him room to turn, and there was a crevice in the rock, into which he backed, concealing half of his body. I was satisfied that he never could get down from his perch. He had reached the place by two prodigious jumps while strong with excitement. A very small projection afforded him a hold to make the last jump, and I thought that he would not dare to come down for fear of missing his footing and being dashed on the rocks far below. And I was right. We had corralled a goat. Cecil beckoned me to come to him. On the way I slipped and fell, the glasses (in the case) dropped from my hand and went bounding down the mountain a hundred yards or more, and striking a boulder, stopped short. "I have no cartridges," said Cecil. I felt in my belt and found one, in the magazine was another. "I have two," I replied, "take my gun and go and kill him."

He hesitated, but I urged him to do so, and laying down his

now useless double barrel, he took my rifle and started up. Gaining the shelf where the goat had run along we followed it to the slippery place, where he was within a hundred yards of the animal. Sitting down and taking a rest he fired. The goat did not move. Once more he fired. The game was unhurt and the last cartridge was gone.

Night was coming on. The last rosy tint had faded from the lofty peaks. Without stopping to look for the glasses we hastened homeward, running at every opportunity. On the way Cecil tried to explain why he had missed the goat. He had never before shot at an animal and I knew from his words that he had had a bad case of "buck fever;" I knew just how it was for a long time ago I had "been there myself." Arrived at camp, we ate a hearty supper, and then Cecil related the events of the day to an interested audience, and I may say a gentlemanly one, for they never once laughed nor sneered at him. How much more pleasant this is than to come into camp after an unlucky day, tired and worn out, and be joked and jeered by the other members of the party. I have noticed that those who indulge in this are themselves unskillful hunters and poor shots. The true hunter is always more considerate and never makes sport of others' misfortune.

In the morning we started again up the creek, accompanied by the Governor and Jack. As soon as we got out of the pines I could see the goat just where we left him the previous evening. We now walked leisurely along, and in due time Cecil reached the spot where he had fired the last cartridge the night before. Bang! went his gun, and the goat fell from his perch and came whizzing down, striking a ledge now and then, and finally stopped short. The great height from which he fell broke every bone in his body. His skull was as soft as a ball of putty; the horns were hanging to the skin on the back. The hide was not injured. One ham only of all the meat was fit to eat. With these I returned to camp, while the others went up toward the head of the basin. I found camp deserted, and, after pegging out the hide, I took a cold bite and stretched out for a snooze. The Colonel and Joe came in about

4 o'clock. They had been up toward the Goat Mountain, but had seen nothing more than tracks. Just before sunset I took the glasses, which had been recovered, and seated myself on the lake shore to take a view of the surrounding country. The first thing that met my eyes after adjusting them was a band of three goats directly opposite, just above the timber and in a small basin. I called out to the others, and we watched them until too dark to see, not forgetting to take a survey of the surrounding country to find the best route to them. Expecting the hunters in any moment, we waited until 8 o'clock before we had supper, and after another hour had passed without sight or sound of them, we turned in and were soon asleep.

Early the next morning, just as we had breakfast ready, the belated ones came in, bringing a goat hide with them. After I left them they had gone to the head of the valley, and, after sitting around an hour or two, saw a band of goats high up, right under a glacier. They figured around a long time trying to get near them, but found no place where they could climb. As last resort they fired at the band at long range, and Jack killed one. They did not have far to go then to get it, for it fell 550 yds. (at least that was the elevation of Jack's gun sight) and landed almost at their feet, a shapeless mass of flesh and bones. Yet the hide was not spoiled. I believe there is no American ruminant except the buffalo which has as thick and tough a skin as the goat. By the time they had the skin off it was dusk, and when they reached the timber it was dark and they could travel no further, so they made a fire and stayed there till daylight. We fried some of Cecil's goat for breakfast. As the steaming odor rose from the pan somebody hinted that there were muskrats around camp. Every one tasted of it, as in duty bound, but that was all. It was tough and strong flavored.

Not only was our little band of goats still in sight, but during the night its numbers had been augmented by one. Of course, those who had been out all night did not feel like hunting, so the Colonel, Joe and I took one of the boats and quickly crossed the lake. The traveling was steep but good, the pines being open and the footing rocky, with a thin layer of dead needles on top. We went very leisurely, stopping now and then to rest, and in two and a half hours sighted the goats. Crawling up to within 250 yds. of them, we sat down behind a couple of scrub pines and watched them a couple of hours. They seem to be very restless animals. They would feed a few minutes, paw a bed in the shade, lie down, get up again in a few minutes and go to feeding. To reach choice bunches of moss they would stand on their hindlegs, their front feet against the rock wall. In shape and action they are much like the buffalo bull. Their long beard gives them a melancholy appearance, and when they sit down on their haunches they are the most ludicrous-looking animal imaginable. While we were watching them another goat came down the steep mountain side and joined them. They seemed to think this an intrusion. One stepped out, deliberately smelled of the new comer, backed off, running up sideways gave him a butt and then struck at him with his front feet. The new comer didn't mind this a bit, but butted and struck back. Then they would stand for some minutes looking sideways at each other mostly surlily and repeat the performance. After sparring thus with two of the goats the newcomer was left alone and they all began to feed together. Meanwhile we had eaten our lunch and wanted to smoke, so we decided to kill or scare, and then fill the pipes. In full sight of the goats, and one especially which had lain down head toward us, we crawled up another hundred yards. The Colonel sat down, placed a handful of cartridges in his hat before him, and taking deliberate aim, fired and wounded one, which hobbled toward us. The Colonel downed him with another shot, and opening his gun, the extractor dropped out. While hunting for this the other goats ran back and forth, and Joe commenced shooting at them. Every time a bullet struck the rocks they would jump away from the place as if they thought that was what was after them. Joe wounded one, and the rest, at last satisfied that something was wrong, struck a shambling trot, disappeared behind a ledge and struck up the mountain. The wounded goat had a broken hindleg, but kept hobbling round the basin and ascending. Joe tried to follow him but found the climbing too dangerous. When we left the basin we could see him standing on the opposite side, more than a gunshot above us. We arrived at camp about 4 o'clock and found dinner waiting us, and our success was related between bites.

The others had slept most of the day. The Governor had caught a fine lot of trout which averaged 2½ lbs. When they heard the sound of our guns they got out the glasses and saw the goats going up over the mountain. The next morning broke dark and windy. Soon after breakfast, the Governor and Jack started for *Natoye tuppo* and Cecil and I for Goat Mountain, leaving the Colonel and Joe in camp. We soon returned, however, as we found the wind too strong to climb with safety. About noon the others came in, bringing the hide and meat of a young doe or nanny goat. This animal was the stupidest of all. Emerging from the pines they saw her about 100 yds. away, standing on a ledge. The goat saw them, too, and instead of running away it lay down out of sight. Laying down his gun Jack ascended to the ledge, walked up close to it and hallowed and waved his arms. The goat rose up, its hair bristling forward like an angry dog's and acted as if it wanted to fight. Then Jack began throwing rocks at it and finally drove it in sight of the Governor, who put a bullet through it.

After dinner some of us got into one of the boats and rowed up to the head of the lake. An excellent view of the valley can be had from the water. For about eight miles it is heavily timbered and about two miles wide, then a round, flat-topped mountain rises from the center and the valley branches to the right and left. Three or four miles further on is the head of each fork, the streams flowing from them forming the headwaters of the St. Mary's. This flat-topped mountain is covered with pine, and is the only one in the country covered with timber. Leaving the boat, we strolled up the valley a mile or two, following the course of the stream. We tried fishing, but did not get a rise. The water is milk-colored at the depth of a foot, bottom cannot be seen, perhaps trout will not stay in such water. We saw several fresh elk signs, and found where some moose had yarded the previous winter. Guided by the sound, we came to a very pretty set of falls, three in number, the lowest and largest being about 100 ft. in height. The highest and most picturesque fall I have yet seen is one that pours into the valley from a large basin on the right hand side. The stream is a good-sized one, and the fall is not less than 1,000 feet, broken in only two places by projecting ledges.

On the next day Cecil and I rowed down opposite Goat Mountain. We saw some goats and spent the whole day trying to get within range of them, but did not succeed, owing to a high rock wall which effectually barred our way. The Governor and Jack had the same experience, but the Colonel and Joe killed two. They were walking along a ledge when two goats suddenly confronted them. The Colonel killed one and the other jumped down on to another shelf some six feet below and tried to hide. Joe leaned over and shot it, fairly powder-burning the beast.

I will not weary the writer with a further recital of our adventures, which, day in and day out, were pretty much the same as herein narrated.

From our experience with the goat we are led to the following conclusions: First, his eyesight is poor; second, he is clumsy, not near as fleet nor as sure-footed as the bighorn; third, he is, altogether, the stupidest animal we ever hunted. I quite believe Mr. Griffin's story — related in *Forest and Steam* some time ago — that a goat once came and lay down near his camp-fire. The wonder is that he didn't come right up and ask for a plate. We considered the flesh of the female goat very good meat. It is tender and has not the musty odor peculiar to that of the males. The heaviest goat we killed was estimated to weigh 150 lbs.

A War Party

Close under the shadow of a great mountain, by a little stream, the camp was pitched. On either hand the unbroken prairie stretched away a long distance; and far to the eastward, in a vast expanse of plains and level ground, could be seen the three Sweetgrass Buttes. It was a warm summer day and the children were running about among the lodges and playing in the water of the little brook. Groups of men were seated in the shade cast by the lodges, smoking and talking, and everywhere the women were busy tanning buffalo cowskins for new lodges. Near the outskirts of the camp was a small hut or shelter, hemispherical in shape, and thickly covered with cowskins. Two or three women were standing near it, and close by a fire was smouldering. It was a sweat-lodge, and in it were a number of men taking a medicine sweat. If you had drawn near you could have heard the hiss of steam as the medicine man sprinkled water on the red hot rocks; and you could also have heard him praying to the Sun and other gods for the success and safety of the party.

"Hear now, oh Sun," he said. "Listen all above persons. We have built a sweat-lodge as you directed. It is round; inside the ground is flat; above us the lodge arches from all directions; thus do we represent the world, your own, as you long ago directed; and as you further — in the long ago — said should be done, we now purify our bodies for we ask you something. Let us live! Let us survive the perils!

"Even as you sink behind the mountain tops, your children here gathered will depart for war. They will seek to be revenged on our enemies. They will fight our enemies who live in the south. Now hear our prayer. They will leave their relations and friends to make war with our enemies. Pity them these relatives, that they sit not with covered heads in their lodges mourning. Let them go about and say, our young men have gone to make war, and they will soon return with scalps and many horses.

"Hi-yu, oh Sun, look down upon us. Let there be high-growing sage brush to conceal our warriors from the enemy. Teach them to travel like the coyote through tall grass and bushes, and in the low places that they be not discovered by the enemy. Now we have built a sweat-lodge, as you directed, and here we give you presents — even parts of our body — as a sacrifice. Pity us. Let us live. Let us survive."

While the old medicine man was repeating this prayer, the warriors sliced bits of flesh from their bodies as an offering to the Sun. At last the pipe was out and the stones cold, and the women having removed some of the coverings of the lodge the men filed out dripping with perspiration and jumped into the stream to cool off.

The sun had set, and while the western horizon was still aglow with his last rays, the war party silently filed out of the village and headed for the south. Silently, and with bowed heads they turned their backs on all they loved. And as silent and sorrowful their fathers, mothers and wives sat in their lodges with covered heads, for all were thinking of the dangers of the far-off trail and praying for life and success.

From the distant hills came the long mournful howl of the wolf and the quavering yelp of the coyote. Darkness settled over the earth, and above the stars twinkled brightly. The great wolf road[1] was white with starlight. All through the

---

[1]The milky way.

night the little band moved on in single file, without word or jest; and in their lead was the greatest warrior of their tribe, a brave, yet cautious man, powerful of frame, keen-eyed and proud, proud of his skill and name, for among many tribes White Wolf was known and feared. Even the animals in some mysterious way must have learned of his skill with the bow, for from afar the buffalo took fright and thundered away through the darkness; the antelope looked not twice, but hurried away with mighty bounds, and from the reedy lakes the ducks arose with startled quacks and flew off through the night.

At last from the horizon *Epi-su-ahts*[1] arose, and hung in the eastern sky like a ball of fire. Then after a while came the light, and at length the sun arose, and it was day once more. Near by were some thickly timbered buttes, and there in the densest cover the party sought shelter for the day. A large bull elk stood feeding among the brush; too late he saw them approach. Twang! went a bow, and a feathered shaft was buried in his heart. Two men were now chosen to ascend the hill and keep a sharp lookout for enemies, and the rest cut up the elk and retired into the thick timber. By a little spring they built a fire and cooked some meat, and having finished eating they rolled up in their robes and went to sleep. At noon the leader awoke and sent two men to relieve those who were watching, and again laid down. As the sun approached the mountain tops, one by one the little party arose and washed in the cold spring. Then they cooked more of the elk, and, as darkness settled over the land, they put on their war sacks and pouches of pemmican, slung their quivers and shields, and once more struck out over the broad prairie.

Now at daylight of the third day they came to the Big River (Missouri) where Pile of Rocks River (Sun River) empties into, and they had no fresh meat. True, each one carried a little pouch of berry pemmican and *depouille*, but that was kept for a time when perhaps they dare not build a fire, or when they might be surrounded by the enemy. Close by the river a large bull was feeding, and he looked fat. Then said

---

[1] Early riser—morning star.

White Wolf: "A fat cow would be better, but now the sun has already risen, and perhaps even now some enemy is watching us; let us hurry, then, and kill this bull. And he crept near and shot an arrow into him; but the bull never raised his head, he kept on walking slowly toward the river, stopping now and then to eat a bunch of grass. And all were much astonished. Again White Wolf shot an arrow into him, and then they all shot him, but still he paid no attention to them. Now he reached the shore and waded slowly out deeper and deeper, and finally sunk out of sight. " *Su-ye stum-ik! Su-ye stum-ik*[1] " they all cried; "we could not kill him; he is one of the fearful kind," and they were afraid. And some said it was a bad sign and wanted to return home, but White Wolf would not let them. "True," he said, "it is not good for man to see these strange and fearful animals. But what we have seen is done—it cannot be helped. Let us now place the watch on two hills, and we will build a sweat-lodge. We will purify our bodies and sacrifice to the Sun," and they did as he said. And after they made the lodge and given the sacrifice, White Wolf called the watchers down, and they went down the river below the place of high falling water, and they shot a blacktail deer and cooked and ate until all were satisfied. Then they dragged down to the river's edge logs which had been left dry by the high waters, and they lashed them together with their lariats; on top of them they piled sticks, and last on top of all they placed their clothes, their water sacks, pouches and weapons, and pushing the raft into the water each one grasped the legs with one hand and swam with the other, and swimming thus, they crossed over to the other side. It was now long past the middle of the day and all were very tired, so White Wolf said: "We will rest here until another night, and I will watch until dark," and he sat up on the bluffs alone to watch, and the rest went into the thick willows and slept.

Now on the seventh day they came to the Yellow River (Judith), and they found a broad trail where many people and horses and travois had lately passed going east, and then

---

[1] *Su-yu-stum–ki*, under the water bull. Supposed to live in the water and to belong to the under-water people.

they were glad, for they knew they were near the enemy. Crossing the Yellow River they crossed over a little point of land and came to the Warm Spring River, and here they rested for the day, two of them going on to a high butte to watch.

Soon one of the watchers came back and awakened them, saying "Uneasy the animals, a band of buffalo run toward the south, and also many antelope, running swiftly as if much scared." Then all arose and cautiously ascended the hill, and they looked carefully in all directions. The day was uneasy, the buffalo were running one way and another, ravens and eagles flew about screaming, and croaking, a band of wolves came sneaking into the river bottom, and last they saw many persons on horseback riding swiftly east. "Ah," said they, "there they are; a war party perhaps, or may be returning hunters."

"Their lodges may not be far off," said White Wolf. "To-night we may arrive there; let us sleep again," and while some watched the others rested until the sun had gone out of sight beyond the mountains. Then they ate a little of their pemmican and took the trail to the east; traveling fast. Near daylight they came almost to It-fell-on-them-Creek[1] (Armells).

"On this creek," said White Wolf, "I am sure they are camped. It is now too late for us to do anything to-night so let us turn up to the mountain and build a war lodge,[2] for we are now in the midst of danger. So they went high up on the side of the mountain in the thick timber, and by a little spring they built the lodge. First they put up the poles — many of them and close together — and over these they placed balsam and spruce boughs in thick layers so a fire could be built inside and yet no light be seen from the outside; and while they were making it White Wolf went out and killed a deer. Then inside they built a little fire of dry quaking asp, and

---

[1]So named because once a number of women were digging natural paint in a cut bank, when the earth gave way above, and many of them were buried beneath it. Many of them being killed the name of the creek in Blackfoot is *Et-tsis-ki-ots-op*.

[2]In Blackfoot *ap-im-an* — sit inside place.

cooked pieces of the deer, and after they had eaten White Wolf went up the mountain to a ledge of rocks to watch while the others slept.

Far below him in the valley he could see the lodges of the enemy. Two hundred and ten he counted, and he saw great herds of horses feeding on the hills close by them. And he looked carefully at the hills, the coulees and ridges, to know which way would be best to approach the camp. "Listen, oh Sun!" he prayed; "make me of good sense. Let my eyes be keen and my arm strong. Let me take many scalps of those men; let me drive away many of their horses."

At sundown they ate a little of the deer and then they opened their war sacks and put on their war headdresses of eagle feathers, and their war shirts of fine buckskin, painted with strange animals and decorated with fine fur, and they painted their faces. Then White Wolf filled a pipe, and they smoked to the Sun and prayed, and each one gave a present to the Sun, and when it was dark they went down the mountain and traveled toward the lower ridges near the camp. Very slowly and cautiously they crept along, keeping in the coulees and low ground. They were now near the camp. The firelight showed dim and red through the lodge skins, and from the smoke holes streams of sparks arose in the still night air. Dogs barked, horses whinneyed, there was a loud confused hum of sounds, people talking, singing, children shouting and laughing, drums beating, the mourning of some for the dead, the loud shouted call to a feast — all this they heard as they neared the camp. And now, close to them they could see shadowy outlines of some horses and hear them eating. Then they took their lariats and caught each one a horse, and these they led, slowly and silently driving the others ahead of them away from camp; and when they had got some distance away they stopped, and leaving the four youngest warriors to guard the horses and keep them from straying away, the others went back. Cautiously they approached the outskirting lodges. In one were seated many persons, for they could see their shadows on the new lodge skins. It was perhaps the lodge of a chief, and there were feasting warriors and principal men. The war party came close to the lodge, most of them stood on each side of the doorway and a few stood round behind it. Then raising his hand to his lips White Wolf sounded the war cry of his tribe. Shrill and loud it echoed through the still night air and was heard by all the people. It made the mother's heart beat, as she grasped her little child in her arms. Young and old were filled with terror. The warriors grasped their weapons and rushed forth into the darkness.

Now from the Chief's lodge the feasters poured out the doorway, but as fast as they came White Wolf and his warriors shot them down and scalped them, and the rush for the doorway was so sudden that those behind could not get out, so they cut slits in the back of the lodge that they might get out unperceived, but even there the enemy struck them down, and the air was filled with war cries, and groans, and shouts for help. Then came warriors hurrying from all parts of the camp, and White Wolf cried out, "Enough, run," and they ran swiftly and disappeared in the darkness, and the Crow warriors followed them but a little way, for they could not see them in the dark, and all know it is foolish to chase a person in the dark, for he can stoop in the grass or hide behind a bush without being seen, and so can shoot down the pursuer when he comes along. So the Crows returned to their camp and from afar the Piegans heard the great mourning, wives and children, fathers and mothers crying for their dead; and the warriors shouted war songs and prepared to follow the enemy when day should come.

Now White Wolf and his warriors came to the horses, and mounting, they rode swiftly away, driving the many loose horses before them, and when they had gone some way they fired the prairie to hide their trail. All through the night they rode, stopping now and then to change horses, and when the sun rose they stopped by a little creek to rest and eat. All through the day they rode, traveling east, and when the sun was getting low they came to the Big River, near the place the Bear River (Musselshell) joins it, and they crossed to the other side. No, not all of them crossed; there in the deep, dark water live the *Su-ye-tup-pi* (under water people), and they took the chief. White Wolf was riding a large strong horse, and when in the middle of the river they both sank slowly out of sight. They reappeared, and the horse made some powerful lunges to escape, but again they sank beneath the water and were seen no more."

"White Wolf has sunk," the others cried. "The *Su-ye-tup-pi* have seized him," they cried, they sat down and mourned for him. Then after a time they went along the shore, thinking perhaps to find his body, and when night came they turned out their horses and built a little fire in the timber and rested. But their hearts were sad; they could not eat; they sat around the fires in silence and mourned. By and by, far off they heard a horse whinny; again and again, nearer and nearer, and then they heard the tramp of his feet. Nearer and nearer and then there was a voice saying "Are you there, my brothers?" Then what a shout went up. What a glad cry was there in the night, and they rushed forth to embrace their friend and leader, who had returned to them.

"Strange, strange have been my adventures," said White Wolf. "You saw me sink under the water and you thought I was dead. So did I. I felt my horse sink beneath me, and I tried to rise, but something held me down. My ears rung. The water strangled me, and then I found myself in a great lodge, and in it were sitting two old people — a man and his wife. They were very small and their hair was thick and long. Then I knew the *Su-ye-tup-pi* had caught me. Said that old man: 'Sit down my son, and let us eat,' and his wife placed before me a piece of turtle and some small lizards. But I could not eat them; you know they are fearful things that we may not touch or eat, and I was afraid. 'You do not eat, my son,' said the old man. 'Why not?'

"'Pity me, I said, 'I am of the prairie people and such as this we greatly fear. We may not touch such food.'

"'Ah,' he said, 'I forgot; our food is not the food of the land people, yet one thing we have you like,' and then placed before me four strawberries.

"'How queer,' I thought, 'only four berries, and I could eat many handfuls.' But I ate one and looked around. The lodge was new and made of strange material. There were parfleches of fish skin, their robes were of otter, bowls they had of turtle shell, and many strange things I saw in the lodge. Then I took another berry, but instead of three, there were four remaining; and when I finished the Old Man took the four and put them away.

"Then said the Old Man to me, 'From what direction comes my son?' And I told him all, of our going to war, and I showed him the scalps.

"'Give me one,' he said; and I gave it, and my shield, that I also gave him. Then said he, 'My son, you have given me presents. You shall live. You shall return to your people; but after this, you and all your tribe must not cross the rivers until you have given us presents. When you reach the shores throw into the water something for us, and you shall cross safely over. But if you do not this, we will take a person and you will see him no more. And now I have said. Shut your eyes and I will lead you to the shore.'

"Then I did as he said, and he took my hand and led me out and up through the water. Soon I felt the water part. I breathed again. I opened my eyes and I stood upon the shore. Close by fed my horse. There was still a little light. I found your trail and followed on."

In the camp of their people the absent warriors were not forgotten. Often the Bear Man unrolled the sacred pipe and prayed for their safe return. Often he stood outside his lodge and shouted their names. And everyday, as evening came he mounted a horse and rode slowly through the camp shaking a medicine rattle, singing a war song and shouting out their names. Thus were the absent ever in the minds of the people.

One day far out on the prairie were seen a band of swiftly-moving objects at times half hid by the clouds of rising dust. Nearer they came. Hark! Listen to the war song! See! It is our absent warriors; they return with many horses!

And all the people went out to meet them, singing loudly the war song with glad hearts, and shouting out the warrior's names. Then was there great joy, and to their relatives the warriors gave many horses, and to those who had lost by death from the enemy a scalp was given; and they danced the scalp dance and were comforted.

J.W. Schultz

To Tan A Hide

The first step in tanning a hide is to flesh it; that is, to remove all fat and flesh from the skin. In the case of a small skin—that of a fox, mink or marten—this is best done bit by bit with a sharp knife, but when the skin is large and tough a flesher is the instrument to use. The back of a drawing knife will be found to do the work as well as a regular fleshing knife. The best time to flesh a skin is soon after the animal has been killed and before the hide is dry. However, if it is not convenient to do it then, dry the hide, and when ready to tan it throw it into a tub of water for twelve hours or more. But be sure the water is cold, and kept so, or the hair will slip. Now cut a piece of green timber, hard wood if possible, about 6 ft. long and from 6 to 10 in. in diameter. Bore two holes in one end and insert two legs, long enough to bring that end as high as your waist, letting the other end rest on the ground. Remove the bark from the upper side of the log and your fleshing horse is complete. Place the skin on this, hair side down, letting a little of it project over the end. Press against it to hold it in place, and holding the drawing knife firmly, edge up, press the back of it against the hide and push. After you have made a few strokes you will get the knack of it, and if the hide is in proper condition will be able to remove all flesh and fat in a few minutes. If it is an oily skin like a beaver, coon, or woodchuck, sprinkle it liberally with corn meal, sawdust or any other absorbent. If you can not conveniently procure a piece of timber for a fleshing horse as described, a 4x4 in. scantling 6 ft. long, will do, only be sure to round off the corners and oval the top, or you will tear the skin. After fleshing, dry the hide before proceeding to tan it.

Here is a recipe for tanning which I have found to be reliable. The quantity is for a hide the size of a domestic sheep. Use more or less as the skin you wish to tan is larger or smaller. First soak the skin thoroughly. Take of borax, saltpeter and glauber salts one/half ounce each, and dissolve in enough warm water to allow it to be spread on the skin. Double it, flesh to flesh, and keep in a cool place twenty-four hours. Second, wash the skin clean. Melt slowly together in a little water, 1 oz. sal. soda, 1½ oz. borax, and 2 oz. refined soap, being careful not to let it boil. When cool enough to bear the hand in it, apply the mixture to the skin, fold as before and keep in a warm place twenty-four hours. Third, wash the skin clean, wring as dry as possible, and place in enough warm rain water to well saturate it, in which 2 oz. of saleratus has been dissolved. Now dissolve 8 oz. common salt and 4 oz. alum in hot rain water, and when cool enough not to scald, place the skin in it for twelve hours. Then wring it out and dry it, at the same time pulling and stretching it. Do not use pumice stone or sandpaper. The last stage of this process is the most important, i.e., the drying. If it is a deer or other hide not easily torn, stretch a stout cord or wire perpendicularly and rub the skin back and forth over it vigorously every few minutes until perfectly dry. Do not let the skin dry too fast: a temperature of 80 degrees is about right.

The Blackfoot Indians tan small skins, such as a fox, lynx, coyote, mink, etc., by a very simple process. After the skin has been fleshed and dried, they rub it well with fresh liver and lay it away for a few hours where it will not dry out. The liver is then scraped off and the skin rubbed with white clay moistened with a little water (This part of the process is not absolutely necessary, the clay merely giving the skin a white, clean appearance), and then the tanner proceeds to dry it, holding it at intervals near the fire, but spending most of the time until it is dry working, twisting and rubbing it. This method makes a very soft tan.

I think the Blackfoot method of fleshing large skins better

than the one I have described. They use an iron instrument shaped like a cold chisel, only twice as wide; small nicks are filed in the edge of it. This flesher can be made of hard wood or bone and will do the work nearly as well as the iron one. They throw the skin over a short post or stretch it out on the ground. Beginning at a place where the skin is quite fleshy, they start it with a knife, and grasping the started point of flesh with the left hand, strike between it and the skin with the flesher a sharp downward blow which still further loosens the flesh as the blows continue in an ever-widening strip.

These people, when tanning large skins (with hair or fur on), first remove one-half the thickness of the hide by "chipping" it with an instrument made of a piece of elk antler, to one end of which a sharp piece of steel is attached. It is, in fact, a miniature hoe. This chipping removes the part of the hide which is the hardest to tan, as it contains the most glue. It is an operation requiring a great deal of practice and skill to do well. In the old days the young girls used to chip pieces of bull hide for practice and never worked on robes until they understood the business. For tanning, these Indians use a mixture of boiled brains, marrow grease and pounded roast liver. This is liberally spread on the hide and allowed to dry in. The hide is then well rubbed with fat, dampened with warm water, rolled up and laid away for a day, when the final process of drying is done; they expose the skin to the sun, or if in winter hang it before the fire, and every few minutes give it a thorough rubbing over a rawhide strand. This is the buffalo robe tan and the only tan which insured a soft robe. White men have tried to tan buffalo robes, and by many different processes, but they could never equal the Indian way of doing it.

In conclusion, my advice to the amateur tanner is this: Send your skin to a furrier and let him tan it for you, but if you are bound to do it yourself, use the first recipe for any skin larger than a fox, and the Indian process for anything smaller.

J.W. Schultz
Piegan, Mont.

Montana Game, Wild and Tame

PIEGAN, Mont., Aug. 26[1] — The shooting season in this state opened August 15. Grouse of all kinds are more numerous than they have been for some years, especially the dusky and sharptail varieties. I for one do not understand why they should be plenty one season and scarce another. The weather apparently has nothing to do with it here. The past spring was very cold and backward, with gales of sleet and snow, which should have had the effect of chilling the young birds to death.

As yet there has been no hunting in the mountains this season. The attractions of the World's Fair,[2] together with the hard times, have caused most sportsmen to forego their annual outing in the Rockies. As a consequence the guides are dejected, and the grizzly is roaming about in happy security, and the white goat squats on the lowest shelf of the mountain.

The employees at the Blackfoot Agency have a number of interesting pets. Mr. Callahan has a badger which is the cutest as well as the clumsiest thing I ever saw. It is now three-fourths grown and as playful as a pup. It delights to roll about with the dog and visits from house to house every day. When in particularly good spirits it backs away from one, raises its head and laughs. Other pets are a coyote, and

[1] 1893

[2] Columbia World Fair, Chicago, 1893.

two swifts (kit foxes). These are not so tame as the badger, but will come up to one for food and can always be seen at the door about meal time.

At Mr. Kipp's ranch the other day I saw a tame wolf which the boys had clipped in imitation of a lion. They left the long hair on the neck and a big tuft at the end of the tail, which gave the animal a very grotesque appearance.

Mr. Irving Cooke, Dr. Martin and several others spent a few days at St. Mary's Lake last week. Mr. Cooke was on Kootenai Mountain one day hunting sheep and would have killed one had he left his horse behind. He was leading the animal along, making considerable noise, when a big ram jumped up in front of him. Mr. Cooke had a snap shot and missed. The sound of the fun scared twenty or more sheep not far away, and they lost no time in getting around the mountain.

Some fine fish were caught in the lake and river by the party, including lakers, Dolly Varden and red-throated trout. The largest Dolly Varden weighed 4 lbs., and was caught by Mr. Cooke. Dr. Martin got the largest laker.

Dr. Walter B. James and Dr. Draper, of New York, are expected here the 30th for a month's outing. Wm. Jackson[1] will guide them. They are going up Cut Bank River and across the summit, where game is very plenty. Their main object, however, in going there, is to scale a certain mountain known as "Flinche's Peak."[2] Dr. James attempted the ascent last season, on the north side, but some perpendicular walls headed him off. He thinks now that by trying the south side he may be able to reach the summit.

Antelope are said to be very plenty in the Sweet Grass Hills. Since the Indians settled down on their reservation no one has hunted them, and as a consequence they are increasing every year.

---

[1]William Jackson was a grandson of the legendary Hugh Monroe and the subject of Schultz's book *William Jackson, Indian Scout*.

[2]This is Flinsch Peak, located on the Continental Divide, between Cutbank Pass and Dawson Pass, both in Glacier Park.

Montana Doings

PIEGAN, Montana, Oct. 24[1] — The water fowl have been going south in immense flocks for the past ten days, and the flight is nearly over. Capt. Cooke, Dr. Martin and the writer were out a few hours last evening and bagged twenty-five geese, five ducks and twelve sharp-tail grouse. Twenty-one of the geese were wavies (*Chen hyperborea*) and four were the rare Ross's goose (*Chen rossi*).

In comparing these four I find that the warts on the base of their bills are of irregular size and shape, no two birds having them alike. When going north or south, to or from their breeding grounds, these geese are always found mixed with the wavies, and never in flocks by themselves. They seldom alight in the lakes here, preferring the open prairies, where they eat the tender shoots of the prairie grass. They, of course, do go to the lakes for water, but only remain in them a few minutes.

John Monroe[2] came in yesterday from the headwaters of Badger Creek, and brought with him the head of a very large

---

[1] 1893.

[2] John Monroe was the eldest son of Hugh Monroe, the legendary white Blackfoot. Born around 1820, he died about 1908.

bull moose which he killed up there. He says there are quite a number of elk, deer and bear in that vicinity, and is going back there to-morrow to have another hunt. Monroe is said to be the best moose hunter in the Northwest. In the early days, when he was employed by the Hudson's Bay Co., way up in the Saskatchewan country, he was far and away the most successful hunter of this game. He is getting pretty old now, and his eyesight is poor, yet it seems he still knows how to "get there."

No one in this country, Indian or white, knows how to call moose, and they are not much hunted. As near as I can learn, Monroe finds the track, and then instead of following it he keeps circling until he locates the animal.

Our Indian police and several employees of this agency had a hunt after a band of train robbers the other day. They were a desperate set of men and killed one white man and wounded one policeman. A party of Kalispel people were also out after the robbers, and as they had a reporter with them, the press despatches gave them all the glory of the affair. I take pleasure in stating here that Wm. Jackson,[1] well known to many *Forest and Stream* readers, was the leader of our party, and chased the robbers up over the summit of the mountains, exchanging shots with them every few minutes. Jackson drove them so fast that they had no time to rest, and finally the men were headed off by the Kalispel party, two of them killed and two captured.

---

[1]Jackson was a grandson of Hugh Monroe, and the subject of Schultz's book *William Jackson, Indian Scout*, Houghton Mifflin, 1926.

Little Plume's Dream

One spring the Blackfeet were camped on the Judith River, which in their language is named the Yellow Stream. Game was getting rather scarce in the vicinity of camp, so it was determined to move camp to Armell's Creek, another tributary of the Missouri, some thirty miles east. At that time I was living with Little Plume, a young warrior of thirty years or more, very brave and a great hunter. He was of a cheerful disposition, always laughing and joking; but the morning we were to move the camp he seemed to be unusually quiet. He got up and had his customary plunge in the river, and ate his breakfast, speaking very little, and seemed to be in deep thought. After a time he got out his war sack, and selecting a bunch of choice eagle's tail feathers — very highly prized by the Blackfeet for decorative purposes — he went out and gave them to the sun; that is, he made a prayer to the sun for health and safety, and concluded by tying the bunch of feathers to the branch of a tree as an offering to the powerful god. Soon the lodges were taken down, everything was packed up and loaded on to the horses, and the march began. In those days a tribe of Indians on the march presented a stirring scene. Most of the riding horses were decked with fancy beadwork and bright saddle trappings; the pack horses carried queer-shaped sacks and pouches of rawhide, which were painted with quaint designs in bright colors. The horses which carried the property of the medicine men, sacred and mysterious bundles, were always white, and their manes and tails were painted with vermillion. The medicine pouches, made of white rawhide, were beautifully painted, and the long fringes of buckskin depending from them nearly to the ground. The costumes of the people added not a little to the brightness of the scene. The older people often wore a buffalo robe or sombre-colored blanket, but the young and middle-aged men and women wore fancy-colored blankets of every conceivable hue; and as they trooped along laughing and chattering, their long hair flying in the breeze, they were an interesting sight. At the head of the column rode the chiefs and head men, followed by the women and children; behind them and on the flanks rode the great body of the warriors driving the loose horses before them, and of these there were many hundred.

As we rode along this bright spring morning, Little Plume informed us that he had a very bad dream. He said that a little old white man came to him and cried out "Beware! You will be in great danger to-morrow."

"How?" asked Little Plume.

"I may not tell you," replied the white man. "All I can say is, have courage, do your best and you may come out all right."

I had never argued with these people about their beliefs. In fact, to get at their inner life, to learn their inmost thoughts and ways, I pretended to be a true disciple of their religion. I made them think that I too, was a sun worshipper and a believer in dreams and signs. Often I would recount to the old men some dream I pretended to have had, and ask their opinion as to its portent. So when Little Plume recounted his dream to me, I said: "My friend, this is truly a fearful dream. How did the little old white man look?"

"He was very small and thin," he replied, "and his face was very smooth and white."

"Well," said I, "if I were you I would be very careful to-day. Stay close to camp, also don't ride any wild horse or fool with your gun. You can't tell what danger your dream has warned

Schultz and son, Lone Wolf, 1894.

—Courtesy of Archives, Montana State University Libraries

you of. There are more ways of being killed than by the enemy. Your horse might fall and crush you; your gun might go off accidentally; a rattlesnake might bite you. Oh, yes, you must be very careful."

"I am not, I never have been," replied Little Plume, "a coward, you know my record in war; it speaks for itself. But I hate these warning dreams. You are told that something is to happen to you, but do not know what it is; and that makes the heart uneasy. You can not eat or talk of anything. Always you are on the watch and fear you know not what."

About 2 o'clock we reached some pine buttes, and while the camp halted to rest a little, Three Suns, the head chief, Little Plume and I rode up to the top of the buttes to take a survey of the surrounding country. Only a few miles distant was the valley of Armell's Creek, very broad and level and bordered by high hills and bluffs. Here and there along the stream were small groves of cottonwood and poplar, and on the hills grew scattering pines. But what interested us most was the game. I got out my glass, a powerful telescope, and by its aid I could see countless herds of buffalo and antelope. Some few of these were between us and the creek, but the main body of them were on the plains west of it. For at least thirty miles, as far as the eye could reach, the prairie was fairly covered with buffalo.

"This is rich country," I remarked, as I handed the glass to Little Plume. "We will soon be feasting on boss ribs."

"I'm glad of that," said Three Suns, "I'm tired of elk and deer meat," and he went on to speak of the buffalo, saying that they really were the life of the Indian, that they were the food, shelter and raiment of the people.

Little Plume, who in the meantime had been sweeping the country with the glass, here, exclaimed that there seemed to be a commotion among the game far down the valley. Some buffalo and antelope had been frightened and were running toward us.

"Well," said Three Suns, "that is nothing strange. You know Running Rabbit's camp (another Blackfoot chief) is between us and the big river (Missouri), and very likely they are camped somewhere about here."

"No," replied Little Plume, "I don't think it was they who frightened the game, for they would be on horseback and we would see them. I feel quite certain that some war party on foot is sneaking along the creek and that they are what scared the game."

"You may be right," said Three Suns, "and it's best to look out. We will herd the horses in for a night or two and keep a strong guard on the watch. Now, then, we ought to be going. I think we shall camp pretty well up on the stream in order not to disturb the game until we are ready to make a big killing. Let us make to the left of that sharp butte over there (pointing to one southeast of us) and keep straight in the direction until we strike the creek."

So we mounted our horses and descended, and shortly the march resumed. In an hour or two we reached the creek and our lodges were pitched on a level bit of prairie handy to wood and water. One of Little Plume's wives (he had five) caught a young antelope which had evidently been born that day and brought it up to us, saying "See what a beautiful little pet I have found."

"I am just hungry for some young antelope boiled," said her brother, who was standing near by, and seizing it, he drew his knife and with one slash ripped it open and threw it upon the ground. The poor thing lay there gasping, and we could see its heart still beating but growing fainter and fainter. It was a brutal act, and I felt like giving the young scamp a good thrashing, but held my peace. The woman roundly berated him, and from the way Little Plume looked I thought he, too, was displeased.

After a hearty meal and a good smoke, Little Plume saddled up a fresh horse, and saying that he was going out on the hills to take a look at the country, rode away. I was tempted to go with him but the day had been a very warm one, and I hardly felt like exercising any more, so I stayed in the lodge and smoked and read (I had quite a bundle of books with me) until it was too dark to see the print. When it was quite dark and Little Plume did not appear, we began to grow quite uneasy about him and after a while the women began to cry and scream that he was killed. I tried to quiet them by saying that he might have found Running Rabbit's camp and concluded to stop there for the night. But it was of no use. So to get away from the doleful noise that they made I went outside. Suddenly I thought I heard a call far out on the prairie, and listening intently I heard it again but could not make out what was said. A young man who was standing heard it too and ran out in that direction. He soon returned, out of breath and so excited we couldn't understand what he said except "Little Plume—almost dead—take him horse." Immediately there was the greatest excitement in camp. Little Plume's wives and female relatives began to mourn, and cry; men came from all directions with drawn weapons, crying out for revenge, and the young man who found Little Plume leading the way, we all went out. When we got up to him we were agreeably surprised to hear him say, though in a very weak voice: "I'm not going to die yet. Put me on a horse and I can ride to camp. I've killed one Sioux." At this there was a wild howl of joy and all began to shout out his name, and those in the camp hearing it, joined in, all crying out in their loudest voices "Little Plume wa! ha! Little Plume wa! ha!" Meaning, the victor. It is the proudest moment of a Blackfoot's life when he thus hears himself extolled by the people.

It did not take us long to get him to camp and in his lodge, and stripping off his leggins we found that he had been shot in both legs; through the calf of one and the thigh of the other. No bones were broken, but the muscles were badly lacerated and there had been considerable loss of blood. I washed the wounds and dressed them with such simple remedies as I had, and after a light meal, our hero was fairly comfortable. Late that night after everything had quieted down, he told me the story of his adventure.

"You remember," he said, "that my dream warned me I would be in danger to-day. He spoke truly; I have had a very close call. All day I have felt uneasy, and the signs have been bad. When my brother-in-law ripped open the young antelope and we could see its heart beating, I felt sure that something was going to happen. Then when I rode away from camp I had gone only a very short distance when the ravens began to circle close to me, and that was still another bad sign. I ought not to have gone out, but I thought I would only go a little way, just to see how the game was and lay out a place for the big hunt to-morrow. I went down the valley quite a little piece, and then started to ride to the top of the bluffs so that I could get a good look at the surrounding country. I was riding quartering up the ridge which is broken by deep coulees, when I saw four buffalo bulls coming toward me up the hill. No other game was close to me, so I drew my horse back out of sight, got off, and crawling to the edge of the coulee, watched for them to come within range. When they were so close I could see their eyes I fired at what I thought was the fattest one, and over he went. The rest ran off. All this time I felt very uneasy. I kept looking up at the top of the hill, then down below. My heart felt heavy, yet I could see nothing to be afraid of. I left my horse and went down and began to cut up the bull. The ravens came all around me, flying close to my head, and calling out, and some lit on the ground so close I could see their eyes. I took out the tongue and then skinned down one side and took out the entrails. Then I got so uneasy I couldn't stand it any longer, and, leaving the tongue and all, I went back to my horse, and had put my foot in the stirrup to get on and ride home, when the thought struck me that I was a foolish coward. I thought of all that fat meat lying there which my children would be so glad to have, and I went back and began to cut off and tie in shape to pack some of the best parts. As I was working away I got very uneasy again, and would often stop and look all around. And I thought I saw something appear for an instant on the edge of the hill above me, but concluded it must have been a raven just flying out of sight. I stooped over to tie some meat, and when I rose up again I saw five Indians where I thought I had seen the raven, and just as I saw them they fired at me. I ran for my horse, and just as I reached him he fell over dead. They had killed him so as to give me no chance to escape. My heart failed me when I saw this, but I ran to a coulee which partly concealed me, and fired three shots at the enemy who were rushing down the hill. That stopped them, and they went out of sight in a coulee. Soon I could see them crawling and sneaking above and below me, and saw they were trying to surround me, so I jumped up, and yelling as loud as I could I ran straight back toward camp. One of the enemy was right ahead of me, and he rose up and fired, but didn't hit me. I stopped and fired, and he threw up his hands, dropped his gun and fell over. I had more courage when I saw this, and felt strong. I ran on as fast as I could, and the enemy followed, shooting pretty often. Every little coulee I came to, I would crouch down and fire a shot at them, which would make them drop down. Then I would run on again. We kept up a running fight this way for quite a while, when a shot struck me in the calf of the leg. It didn't hurt much at first, but I could feel the blood running down into my moccasin. The next coulee I came to I fired twice at them, tore off a piece of my shirt and ran on. At the next coulee, after firing at them I tied up the wound as well as I could, and ran on again. They didn't seem to want to catch up with me, but kept a good long rifle shot behind. I suppose they thought by keeping it long way off and shooting pretty often, they would get me after a while without much risk to themselves, but as I ran I kept dodging this way and that, and gave them a pretty difficult mark. I was getting pretty well toward camp and was running up a hill, when a shot struck me in the thigh, and over I went. I thought then my time had come, but I managed to roll into a little washout. Then I sat up, and fired twice at them. They had started to run toward me, but that stopped them, and they went 'way back and started to climb to the top of the hill. I knew if they should get up there that they would surely kill me, for they would be in easy range and could see me plainly from there. I prayed then. I didn't quite give up. I called on my dream white man for help. I had only three cartridges left, and thought I would save them for the last round. As I was looking up over the edge of the coulee I saw them stop climbing. Soon one of them made a sign to me and motioned me to go home, and that they would go to their home. I didn't answer at all. I just took aim and fired once at them. They turned and ran back the way they had come. I am not sure what made them do this, but think when they were getting near the top of the hill they either saw our camp or some of the people riding about, and thought they would be safer to get back toward the Missouri. As soon as I saw them going I fixed up both my wounds as good as I could, and using my gun for a crutch hobbled toward camp. I thought I would never get here. Toward the last I had to crawl a little way at a time, and when you heard me call I was so weak I could have gone no further."

"Well, my friend," said I, "your dream gave you a true warning, didn't it?"

"Yes," he replied, "it did." "What powerful medicine that little old white man is. I wonder what kind of a white man he really is."

The next day a large party scoured the country in search of the war party (supposed to have been Sioux), with whom Little Plume had the battle, but could not find them. Where he shot one of them they found where he had fallen. The grass was covered with blood and all tramped down. Undoubtedly, his comrades on their retreat had taken him away and buried him, or perhaps sunk the body in one of the deep holes of the creek.